Escape *from* Earth

PETER ACKROYD

LONDON, NEW YORK, MUNICH,
MELBOURNE and DELHI

Senior editor Carey Scott
Senior art editor Stefan Podhorodecki
Editor Matt Turner
Art editor Darren Holt
Managing editor Andrew Macintyre
Managing art editor Jane Thomas
Category publisher Linda Martin
Art director Simon Webb
Production controller Erica Rosen
Picture researchers Jo de Gray, Julia Harris-Voss
DTP designer Siu Yin Ho
Jacket designer Neal Cobourne

Consultant
Peter Bond

First American Edition, 2003

Published in the United States by
DK Publishing, Inc.
375 Hudson Street
New York, New York 10014

04 05 06 07 08 10 9 8 7 6 5 4 3 2

A Cataloging-in-Publication record for this book
is available from the Library of Congress.

ISBN 0-7566-0171-1

Reproduced in Italy by G.R.B. Editrice, Verona
Printed and bound in Italy by L.E.G.O.

Discover more at
www.dk.com

Contents

To escape from Earth and explore the vast Universe from which life originally sprang is one of humankind's most enduring dreams and ambitions.

Early science fiction writer Jules Verne once said that "What one man may imagine, another can achieve," and in the 20th century, his prophecy was to be proved correct. For this was the century of real technological miracles. Within one lifetime it was possible to witness the first airplane flight across the English Channel, undertaken in 1909, and the first orbit of a crewed spacecraft around the Earth, in 1961. In a little over 50 years, humankind had conquered the skies. Outer space was the next frontier. The Earth was reaching out. We had nowhere else to go. The endless and inexhaustible curiosity of our species had left no corner of the Earth unexplored—with the exception of the farthest depths of the oceans—so we looked upward to the immense darkness that surrounded us.

Space travel and space flight were at first thought to be all but impossible. It was comprehensible and reasonable that discoverers such as Christopher Columbus and Francis Drake set sail for unknown lands, since the Earth was a finite and, in many ways, a predictable place. But to send men and women into outer space, where everything was utterly hostile to human life itself—well, it was merely a fancy or a dream. Yet it was no dream. It came to pass.

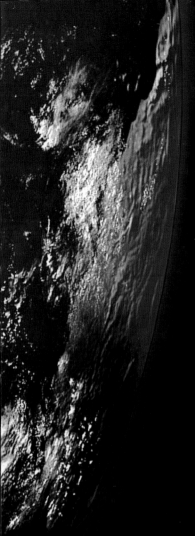

CHAPTER ONE

The Earth
reaches out

Humankind's eternal dream of exploring the planets and the stars was to become a reality in the 20th century. The technology that made it possible was a result of one of the most destructive wars in history, World War II.

The devastating power of the atomic bombs dropped on the Japanese cities of Hiroshima and Nagasaki brought World War II (1939–45) to an abrupt end. A period of time known as the Cold War then began. For 50 years, almost to the end of the last millennium, the empires of the United States and the

Soviet Union—representing the rival political systems of capitalism and communism—were undeclared enemies. There was no actual war between them, although it threatened many times. A state of uneasy peace was maintained because both powers possessed the means to destroy one another utterly. Neither side dared act first. They both continued to develop more and more deadly weapons. The arms race, as it became known, seemed unstoppable. In this feud, missiles carrying nuclear warheads were the obvious weapons of global supremacy; they could leap effortlessly between continents. But technological achievement itself became a matter of fierce competition between the two world powers. The exploration of space afforded many opportunities for military ambition and technological accomplishment. For the Soviet Union or the United States to be the first to land a man on the Moon would be an indisputable symbol of imperial supremacy.

When the Soviet cosmonaut Yuri Gagarin completed one orbit of the Earth in 1961 (see p. 32)—to the delight of the Soviet Union and the deep dismay of the United States—it was considered to be the beginning of a great adventure. This was the start of a grand enterprise in which humankind would escape from its small planet and venture out into the Universe. Where some hoped, others feared. For this was believed to be the beginning of the communist conquest of space, a startling leap in the technology of the Cold War. "I would not like to go to sleep," US vice-president Lyndon Johnson said, "beneath a communist Moon."

Liquid oxygen

Liquid hydrogen (or kerosene)

Oxygen and hydrogen (or kerosene) mix in the combustion chamber, where they ignite.

Thrust launches rocket.

LIQUID PROPELLANT
Rockets fueled by liquid propellant can be controlled by valves that adjust the flow of fuel into the engine.

How a rocket works

Rocket flight is based on the laws of physics, as outlined by British scientist Isaac Newton (1642–1727). One of these laws states that for every action, there is an equal and opposite reaction. When a rocket is launched, the action of the fast-moving gases that are expelled downward from its engines creates an equal and opposite reaction that pushes the rocket upward, just as the air escaping from a balloon propels it forward. The rocket must be traveling fast enough to overcome Earth's gravity and enter orbit.

However, as well as being the beginning of a new era, Gagarin's flight was also the climax of a great, and largely secret, effort of the last century. This had begun in 1903, when a Russian schoolteacher, Konstantin Tsiolkovsky, designed on paper a rocket fueled by liquid hydrogen and liquid oxygen. The world paid little attention until, in 1912, an American scientist named Robert Goddard began a theoretical study of rocket propulsion. It is highly appropriate and significant that the 20th century began with an investigation of space travel, and that those involved were a Russian and an American. In the beginning was the seed of an enterprise that would come to dominate the end of the century.

GODDARD THE PIONEER
Robert Goddard (far left) has been recognized as the father of American rocketry. In the 1950s, American rocket scientists discovered that it was virtually impossible to construct a rocket or launch a satellite without reference to his work.

OFF THE GROUND
Inspired by reading science fiction as a youth, Goddard went on to launch the first liquid-propelled rocket from his aunt's farm in Massachusetts in 1926.

Just after World War I (1914–18), Goddard wrote a book entitled *A Method of Reaching Extreme Altitudes.* To many, his topic seemed an impossible enterprise and a distraction from the repair work needed on the war-torn Earth itself, but by 1926, he had launched the world's first true rocket. It was fueled by liquid oxygen and gasoline and reached a height of 41 ft (12.5 m) at a speed of 62 miles (100 km) per hour. We have no visual record of this historic flight. Goddard's wife, Esther, had brought a wind-up movie camera to record the launch, but she was still winding it at the moment of liftoff. The flight lasted only 2.5 seconds, all of which she missed.

If we compare the nature of Goddard's first rocket, launched in 1926, with that which carried the first space shuttle, launched in 1981 (see p. 98), the incredible speed of progress becomes evident. Goddard's rocket weighed 16 lb (7.3 kg) when fueled; the later shuttle was to weigh 4.4 million lb (2 million kg) fueled. The earlier rocket reached the height of a two-story house, while the shuttle was to reach an altitude of 250 miles (400 km). The speed of the space shuttle was about 270 times greater than that of Goddard's rocket. This extraordinary progress was achieved in a little over 50 years.

In 1924, the Soviet Union founded a Rocket Research and Development Center. This organization manufactured engines uniquely designed for rockets. In 1933—under the leadership of Chief Designer of Rockets and Spacecraft Sergei Korolev—the Soviets sent up two liquid-fueled rockets with the aid of liquid propellant, the second of which reached a height of 262 ft (80 m). In that same year, Konstantin Tsiolkovsky, who was to become known as the "father of space travel," predicted that many Russians would live to see humans in space flight. In this he proved correct. Less than 30 years later, Yuri Gagarin would orbit the Earth in an astonishing feat orchestrated by Korolev himself. The journey away from the Earth is characterized by the extraordinary speed of invention.

In 1927, German scientists established an association named the Society for Space Travel. Among its members was a young scientist, Wernher von Braun, who quickly became a leading figure. From 1933, von Braun and his team were employed by the German army to develop liquid-fueled rockets. They designed a number of rockets known as the A series, which were tested successfully in the years before World War II. These vehicles were capable of carrying payloads of almost 198 lb (90 kg). The payloads were, of course, bombs: the early rockets were weapons.

ROCKET TECHNOLOGY
The space shuttle, first launched in 1981, uses rocket boosters—the successors of Goddard's early rocket—to help it get into orbit.

Sergei Korolev

Born in the Ukraine, Sergei Korolev (1906–66) was responsible for the first satellite launch and the first crewed space flight. In the 1930s, Korolev headed GIRD, a Moscow-based group of rocket enthusiasts who built liquid-propellant rockets. He also led a team at the Rocket Research Institute until, in 1938, under Stalin's dictatorial regime, he was charged with subversion and sentenced to forced labor. Korolev escaped almost certain death when, still a prisoner, he was recalled to work on rocket programs. In 1944, he was released, and became Chief Designer of Rockets and Spacecraft. He died in 1966.

UNTIMELY END
Korolev's sudden death at age 59 was a severe blow to the Soviet space program.

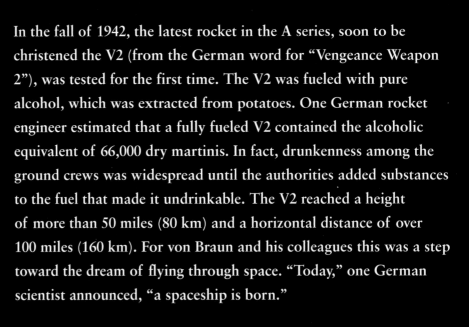

In the fall of 1942, the latest rocket in the A series, soon to be christened the V2 (from the German word for "Vengeance Weapon 2"), was tested for the first time. The V2 was fueled with pure alcohol, which was extracted from potatoes. One German rocket engineer estimated that a fully fueled V2 contained the alcoholic equivalent of 66,000 dry martinis. In fact, drunkenness among the ground crews was widespread until the authorities added substances to the fuel that made it undrinkable. The V2 reached a height of more than 50 miles (80 km) and a horizontal distance of over 100 miles (160 km). For von Braun and his colleagues this was a step toward the dream of flying through space. "Today," one German scientist announced, "a spaceship is born."

But their superiors had other plans. By 1944, the Germans were in grave peril of losing the war, and these newly created rockets were their last chance of victory. German radio had already broadcast the imminent launch of a new and deadly secret weapon that would destroy the enemy. Many people were incredulous at talk of flying rockets, but in the fall of 1944, a V2 was launched against the enemy, exploding in a London suburb. Following the explosion of the warhead, terrified Londoners heard another bang—the sonic boom catching up with the rocket. Over the next few months, until the end of the war, more than a thousand V2s fell on London. But they failed to make the decisive impact the German army had hoped for, and in the spring of 1945, Allied troops began their invasion of Germany. One of their most important targets was von Braun's

V2 FOR VENGEANCE
Although von Braun's dream was to perfect a rocket for space travel, the German military wanted his expertise for their war effort. Here at Cuxhaven on the north German coast, von Braun's V2 long-range missile is prepared for launch against Great Britain.

ATTACK FROM THE AIR
Toward the end of World War II, Germany
began to use V2 rockets as bombs. Frequent
air raids on Great Britain forced Londoners
to take shelter in underground train tunnels.

secret testing facility at Peenemunde on the
Baltic coast. The German authorities had
already issued instructions that von Braun
and his colleagues were to be killed, and
the secrets of the V2 buried with them.
Even if von Braun was not aware of this,
he understood by now that his country was
losing the struggle. He had the foresight
to surrender himself, and many of his

Wernher von Braun

When German-born
Wernher von Braun
(1912–77) was only 16,
he built a complete
observatory. In 1932, at age
20, he began work for the
German army, developing
the V1 and V2 rockets. After
WWII, he and his key staff
were moved to the US,
where they turned the V2
into an intercontinental
ballistic missile. Later, he
produced the Saturn V—the
rocket that put humans on the Moon in 1969. Von
Braun had always hoped to send a crewed mission to
Mars, but after the Moon landings, the funding and
political will for costly space ventures no longer existed.
He resigned his NASA post in 1972.

Walt Disney partnership
*Von Braun worked with Walt
Disney to promote public
interest in space exploration.*

colleagues, to the American military. Von Braun knew that he was a necessary part of the future. The United States knew it, too. So we have the paradox that the man who created death machines for the German army was welcomed by the Allies, the very target of those machines.

As part of a project known as Operation Paperclip, the American authorities transported von Braun, his captured colleagues, some one hundred missile parts, and many tons of paperwork and plans across the Atlantic to the US in September 1945. Here, they began work on developing improved V2 rockets for the American military. A series of V2 rockets was launched from an area in New Mexico known as White Sands. The first was in the spring of 1946 and, over the next few years, there were a number of launches carrying cameras, fruit flies, and even monkeys. One monkey died in 1958 when its return capsule sank in the ocean before it could be recovered, making it the first of the animals to be killed in the name of American rocketry.

White Sands continued to be the center of rocket development. Between 1949 and 1955, a rocket known as the Viking flew high into the atmosphere on 12 separate occasions,

WHITE SANDS
This digital map shows the isolated area called White Sands in New Mexico that provided the site for US rocket research. In August 1945, V2 rocket parts, captured in the war in Europe, were brought here.

FLORIDA TESTS
In July 1950, the launch of a V2 rocket was captured on film at the new Cape Canaveral launch site in Florida.

although on five of these flights, the rocket exploded as a result of various failures. These failures were widely reported, unlike Soviet tests, which were conducted in conditions of the highest secrecy. Developing rockets for space travel was Wernher von Braun's ultimate goal, and in 1960, his team of engineers and scientists would be transferred to the newly created NASA, the National Aeronautics and Space Administration. Under its sponsorship, von Braun was to design and test the Saturn rockets that would take people to the Moon in 1969. One of the great conquests of outer space was the direct result of the bombs that had hit London only 25 years before.

NASA
The National Aeronautics and Space Administration was created in 1958 to carry out research into nonmilitary space activities. These included space transportation, astronomy and space science, and humans in space.

But in 1950, the Moon landing was not yet even conceived. In that year, a launch pad was constructed in a location by the ocean; a desolate part of Florida called Cape Canaveral. The area was known locally as Cocoa Beach, and was part of a peninsula covered by sand, brush and scrubland—unlovely and largely unvisited. Yet since 1950 it has been deemed one of the central elements of the great space enterprise. Almost at once it became known as a boomtown, since the money followed the new technology as irresistibly as rivers flow toward the sea. It is now a great sprawling complex, home to the Kennedy Space Center, and its flat scrub has been replaced by vehicle assembly buildings as vast as the greatest cathedrals.

NUCLEAR DEVASTATION
After the atomic bomb was dropped on Hiroshima, Japan, people were quick to realize the threat of nuclear bombs delivered by the new rocket technology.

The Soviets were not left behind. They built their own city of cathedrals, too—Baikonur Cosmodrome, the largest space center in the world. Construction began in 1955. The site chosen for it was a

vast and mostly uninhabited desert on the harsh steppes of Kazakhstan in the southeastern Soviet Union. It was a monumental project. The construction of the launch pad involved digging the world's largest human-made pit. The first layer of soil was dug with hand tools, and the exhausted men slept outdoors on reed mats until they had built their first living quarters. Local rodents carried plague and cholera and had to be poisoned, but many of the workers were affected by inhaling the toxin, too. The winter temperature plummeted to −40°F (−40°C), while in summer the scorching desert heat forced the men to sleep in wet sheets, which lured scorpions and large spiders in from the dry desert. In spite of these dreadful conditions, work progressed quickly, and in 1957, the Cosmodrome's first launch pads were operational.

Like the Americans, the Soviets had also been intent on acquiring the secrets of the V2 from Peenemunde and, after the war, hundreds of German V2 rocket technicians and draft plans not taken by the US had been shipped to the Soviet Union, and eventually to Baikonur Cosmodrome. With this expertise, Soviet scientists also were able to redesign the V2. By 1957, they had developed the world's first practical intercontinental ballistic missile, with enormous consequences for the progress of the Cold War. The announcement that the Soviet Union had missiles that could reach the United States from the other side of the world caused panic in the US government and accelerated the nuclear arms race.

There had been other developments of a no less interesting, if less startling, nature. In the fall of 1947, an American pilot, Chuck Yeager, became the first person to break the sound barrier—the sonic wall that is penetrated at a speed known as Mach 1, about 750 miles (1,207 km) per hour. Yeager made the flight in a rocket-powered plane known as the Bell X-1. Although forbidden by his cautious controllers to "go supersonic," he decided to attempt it anyway. People on the ground heard an ear-shattering sound: the sonic boom that an aircraft delivers when it is flying faster than the speed of sound. Yeager later remarked on the ease of the ride. After reaching Mach 1, he said, "It was as smooth as a baby's bottom: Grandma could be sitting up there sipping lemonade."

FASTER THAN EVER
An F/A-18 Hornet breaks the sound barrier. The strange cloud is water condensation caused by the shock wave the plane creates as it speeds through the air.

It was a remarkable feat, not least because Yeager had broken two ribs after a horseback-riding accident just days before the flight, but not wishing to be grounded, had kept the injury secret.

Yeager's flight is of significance in the history of space exploration, too, because the X-1's successor, the rocket plane X-15, could actually fly above the Earth's atmosphere and then return with its pilot to Earth. The X-15's development thus contributed to the possibilities of a future reusable space shuttle. But the space shuttle was an idea whose time had not yet come. It waited, as it were, in the wings of space.

Chuck Yeager

Always ready to take a risk, Charles Elwood "Chuck" Yeager (1923–) became the first man to break the sound barrier. Born in West Virginia, he joined the Air Force in 1941 and trained as a fighter pilot. He saw action in World War II, when he was shot down over Nazi-occupied France, but escaped to England before insisting on a return to combat. When the war ended, Yeager trained as a test pilot and was selected to fly in the X-1 program that proved so successful in pushing the boundaries of flight.

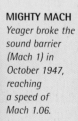

MIGHTY MACH
Yeager broke the sound barrier (Mach 1) in October 1947, reaching a speed of Mach 1.06.

CHAPTER TWO

The space age *begins*

In 1957, the era of space exploration began in earnest. The Soviet Union and the United States began to compete, in what became known as the space race, to become the dominant power in space.

On October 4, 1957, the world's first satellite was launched from Baikonur Cosmodrome. After the launch, the rocket's four booster engines fell away, and it went into orbit around the Earth at a speed of 4.9 miles (7.99 km) per second. Then, after a series of maneuvers, a glittering silver sphere some 23 in (58 cm) in diameter emerged. This was *Sputnik 1*. It was equipped with four aerials and two radio transmitters, and at its highest point it circled the Earth at a distance of 588 miles (946 km). It took a little over an hour and a half to complete each orbit, its signal— beep, beep—becoming, for a few weeks, the most famous sound in the world. Under the supervision of Sergei Korolev, *Sputnik 1* transmitted for 21 days and endured 92 days in space before it fell and disintegrated in the Earth's upper atmosphere. Yet for those weeks *Sputnik*

FIRST SATELLITE
Sputnik 1 was the first satellite to be launched. Shining in space, it was a clear signal of Soviet technological superiority.

shone in space and was watched with wonder by the peoples of the Earth. It also had more prolonged effects. It was the first time in history that any human-made object had transcended the forces of gravity. It was a revelation. It was also a liberation. It offered endless possibilities for humankind. Yet it caused distress as well as amazement in the Western world, particularly in the United States. The Soviets had beaten the US in the game of technology. If they were able to control space, where might they next demonstrate their superiority?

It had not escaped the attention of the American military and political elite that Soviet rocket technology might now be able to deliver bombs to any part of the planet. The communists had, remarked future president Lyndon Johnson, "established a foothold in outer space." Another politician talked of "national extinction." With *Sputnik* bleeping above their

Sputnik 1

The satellite *Sputnik 1* was launched from Baikonur Cosmodrome in the USSR on October 4, 1957. The satellite was an aluminum sphere, 22 inches (58 cm) in diameter, weighing 184 lb (84 kg). *Sputnik 1* circled the Earth at an altitude of 500 miles (800 km), traveling at a speed of 18,000 mph (30,000 kph). It orbited the Earth every 90 minutes. The beeps it emitted from its transmitters were broadcast on radios all over the world, signaling the beginning of the Space Age.

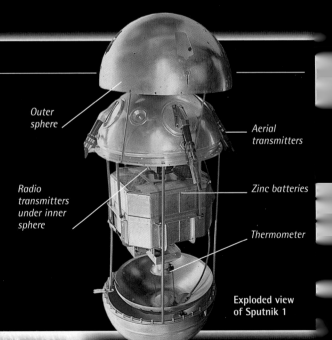

Outer sphere

Radio transmitters under inner sphere

Aerial transmitters

Zinc batteries

Thermometer

Exploded view of Sputnik 1

heads, circling the globe so swiftly and so perfectly, Americans felt trapped.

And so there ensued a frenzy of research, of launches and tests, which became known as the space race. The *New York Times* called it a "race for survival." President Dwight D. Eisenhower realized that this was a race for military prowess, but it was also for a greater prize than that— it was a race to reclaim American national honor. He knew that it would come at a high price, but there was no other national goal that seemed more obvious and more important.

SPACE DOG
A model of Laika, the first animal to orbit the Earth, inside *Sputnik 2*.

The urgency of the situation was emphasized a month after the launch of *Sputnik 1*, when the Soviets launched *Sputnik 2*. This was an even greater achievement by Sergei Korolev. Its size and weight—of more than 1,000 lb (450 kg)—were impressive and astonishing. Here was a great craft voyaging around the planet, as if it had come from a science fiction movie. It was remarkable for two reasons. The satellite contained instruments to test radiation in space, and so marks the first time detailed information was transmitted back to the Earth. But there was an even more astonishing aspect to this flight. *Sputnik 2* was carrying a dog. The animal, a small mongrel named Laika ("Barker" in Russian), was the first living thing to orbit the Earth. She became, for a time, the most famous creature in the world. Alas, she did not survive the experience. It is thought that she died from overheating in the cabin just a few hours after the launch.

SPUTNIK 2 LAUNCH
On November 3, 1957, the satellite *Sputnik 2* was launched by this R-7 rocket from Baikonur Cosmodrome.

The US government tried to reply to these Soviet successes with the launch of the first American satellite, aboard a Vanguard rocket. The Vanguard rockets (successors of the Vikings) were built as part of a program that had been announced by President Eisenhower three years earlier, but now that the space race had begun, there was pressure for faster deployment. Unfortunately, the rocket fell at the first hurdle. It rose a few feet at liftoff, but then fell back and exploded on the launch pad. It was a disaster for the American government, leading to newspaper headlines such as "KAPUTNIK." The US regained some pride with the successful launch of *Explorer 1*, a research satellite, at the beginning of 1958. There was no unfortunate accident on this occasion, and the Jupiter rocket took

SPACE RADIATION
Thanks to satellites such as the Explorers, studies of the Universe's invisible elements—such as radiation—can be made. This modern gamma-ray (radiation) image is of the sky as seen from the Earth. The red horizontal band is the plane of our own galaxy, the Milky Way.

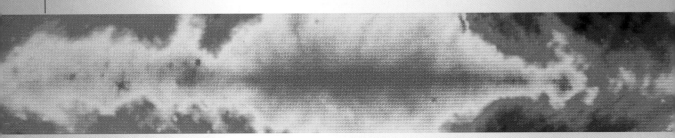

the satellite safely into space. *Explorer 1* was carrying the latest technology, including instruments for measuring high-energy particles that come from the depths of space, known as cosmic rays, and ultrasonic microphones to register the impact of micrometeorites. It also carried Geiger counters to register the presence of radiation and, as a result of this flight, a band of radiation was indeed discovered around the Earth.

There were, in fact, 11 other successful flights in the early Explorer program, over a period of four years, which were used to measure phenomena such as gamma rays (a form of radiation) and magnetic fields. *Explorer 6* managed to photograph parts of the Earth's surface and transmit them back, to be picked up by dish-shaped antennae. The images were blurred and grainy,

VANGUARD DISASTER
The Vanguard rocket was
chosen to launch the eagerly
awaited first US satellite.
Disastrously, it blew up on
liftoff. According to one
observer, the explosion
seemed "as if the gates of
Hell had opened up."

VANGUARD 1 SATELLITE
The launch of *Vanguard 1* on March 17, 1958 was the first success in the Vanguard program. It is still in orbit today.

THE MERCURY 7
The first seven astronauts chosen by NASA were known as the Mercury 7, and they became world-famous. They are, from left to right: Wally Schirra, Alan Shepard, Deke Slayton, Gus Grissom, John Glenn, Gordon Cooper, and Scott Carpenter.

the definition unremarkable, but they were the beginning of a whole new field of human endeavor. If it were now possible to make images of the Earth, with a variety of different instruments, what else might be achieved? It marked, for example, the beginning of proper weather forecasting and the monitoring of the spread of deserts and the destruction of forests, as well as the aerial search for natural hazards such as volcanic eruptions.

Yet these were the early days of space research, when the facts we now take for granted were first being discovered. The excitement and the intensity of the engagement with outer space had only just begun. It was still, of course, fueled by national competition, and in March 1958, a meeting of American politicians, military leaders, and scientists discussed the speediest and most appropriate way of getting a human into space—ahead of the Soviet Union. The result was NASA's first crewed flight program, Project Mercury, which would run for almost five years. In April 1959, seven astronauts, all military test pilots, were selected for Project Mercury.

Discoverer photograph of a Soviet military site

Six weeks after the launch of *Explorer 1*, the satellite *Vanguard 1* was fired into orbit, with the distinction of being the first satellite to carry solar batteries. Theoretically, it could continue to produce electricity until the day (or night) that the Sun dies. This satellite, part of the antiquated hardware of early space exploration, is too high to be drawn into the Earth's atmosphere, where it would burn up. As a result, it has been traveling around the globe since 1958, a functioning record of these first days of space flight.

In December 1958, an Atlas rocket carried into orbit a satellite that was designed to receive and transmit radio messages. Known as *SCORE* (Signal Communications Orbit Relay Experiment), it transmitted messages for two weeks. *SCORE* was the first example of one of the most significant uses of satellites. It was the herald of a revolution in communications that still continues today.

Early in the following year, the US also launched the Discoverer program, in which variously equipped satellites would be sent into space on Thor rockets.

DISCOVERER PROGRAM
This secret program provided US intelligence with film of Soviet military sites, taken by satellite cameras and parachuted back to Earth. Here, a capsule containing film is examined by a technician.

The far side of the Moon, photographed by Luna 3 in October 1959.

LUNA 3
This Soviet probe photographed the far side of the Moon for the very first time. At the time, this was yet another example of superior Soviet space technology.

There were many failures, but the project was of great importance to the American government because of one central fact: it involved the construction of a recoverable reentry capsule. The satellite jettisoned the capsule back to Earth, and continued in its orbit. The capsule, containing ordinary film taken by the satellite's camera, was then recovered. But why was this considered to be so significant? Under conditions of strict secrecy, the American government had used the program to conduct a series of experiments with what have become known as spy satellites. The Discoverer satellites took photographs of the Soviet Union's launch sites and military bases while flying above its landmass, and the film was later rescued and developed on American soil. One of the areas covered by these secret cameras was the Baikonur Cosmodrome, where the activities of Sergei Korolev and his colleagues was the subject of intense curiosity and speculation. Initially, objects smaller than 32 ft (10 m) could not be detected, but by the end of the program in 1972, much smaller objects, less than 3 ft (1 m), could be clearly seen. It was a remarkable development in space technology, and a no less remarkable example of the political use of that technology.

In 1958, the satellite *Sputnik 3* had been launched from Baikonur Cosmodrome as a reminder of what the Soviets could accomplish. Soviet rockets were more powerful than American ones, and so were able to deliver larger, heavier satellites: at 1.4 tons (1.3 metric tons), *Sputnik 3* weighed about 30 times more than its American counterparts. *Sputnik 3* stayed in orbit for almost two years. Then, at the beginning of 1959, Korolev set his sights on the Moon. The first satellite intended to reach the Moon, *Luna 1*, missed its target and went into orbit around the Sun (becoming the first spacecraft to do so), but *Luna 2* was more successful. Deliberately aimed at the Moon, *Luna 2* crashed into its surface on

September 13, 1959, at a speed of 2 miles (3.2 km) per second. It was the first human-made object ever to touch the surface of the Moon.

Although of little scientific interest, the event was a dramatic demonstration of Soviet rocketry, and it made headline news. Just a month later, *Luna 3* photographed the far, or "dark," side of the Moon, which is invisible from the Earth. This was seen as an extraordinary feat of technology. The film was developed and processed in space before being beamed back to the Earth. Here was a landscape that had never before been seen. A lost world came into view. It was almost as if we were seeing images of some inconceivably ancient past, magically conducted through the ether. It seemed to be the clear intent of the Soviets to acquire the space "rights" to the Moon— to keep it, as it were, for itself—but all that was soon to change.

The new decade of the Sixties opened with a rush of satellites. In the spring of 1960, two American satellites with wholly different purposes were launched. The *Transit 1B* was the first American military navigational satellite. It was the first of three series of Transit satellites (each designed to transmit for just three months) that would be used to accurately position the ships and submarines of the US navy. *Tiros 1*, the first satellite in the TIROS (Television and Infrared Observation Satellite) program, was launched in the same season in a bid to assist weather forecasting. *Tiros 1* was able to film cloud formations and, with infrared photography, record heat measurements of the clouds and of the Earth's surface. It returned the first-ever global cloud-cover pictures.

TIROS PROGRAM
Tiros 1, launched on April 1, 1960, was the first satellite in a program designed to develop a 24-hour weather-monitoring system.

In May, the US also dispatched into space a satellite known as *Midas 2*, a missile defense alarm system able to detect the heat traces of a Soviet rocket launch. It failed to perform successfully, but the importance of the project was underlined by the quick launch of *Midas 3* and *Midas 4*. Space was indeed being colonized. In the summer of 1960, *Echo 1* was launched to bounce radio and television signals around the world. It was essentially an aluminum balloon, almost 100 ft (30 m) in diameter, which by intricate and ingenious maneuvers had been inflated in space. Once more the world could watch a satellite in orbit and wonder.

Indeed, outer space had entered the imagination of the world. There followed a host of science fiction movies in which rockets carved traces over alien skies. Shakespeare's play *The Tempest* was staged among the stars in the 1956 movie *Forbidden Planet*. In the 1960s, some of British science fiction writer H. G. Wells's prophetic stories were made into movies, including *The Time Machine* (1960) and *First Men in the Moon* (1964). In Great Britain, the adventures of time-traveling Dr. Who terrified small children and quickly gained a cult audience. There were science fiction comic books and science fiction novels, all of them producing visions of the cosmos for a public consumed by the possibilities of rocket science and space exploration.

ECHO IN SPACE
Inflatable satellite *Echo 1*, launched in 1960, deflated after a few months, although it remained in orbit until 1968.

PURE CARBONIC

In August 1960, the Soviet Union sent up another Sputnik with a remarkable payload. *Sputnik 5* carried two dogs, Belka and Strelka, as well as 40 rats, two mice, and hundreds of insects and plants, into orbit. They stayed in space for a day and were then able to reenter the Earth's atmosphere without visible harm. The space engineers held the dogs up in triumph before the cameras of the world, as living testimonials to the fact that space travel was not necessarily fatal. Other canine passengers were not so fortunate and, a few months later, two dogs were burned to death on reentry into the Earth's atmosphere.

There were other accidents at Baikonur Cosmodrome, but they rarely broke the cover of Soviet silence and secrecy. The worst of these was in October 1960, when a rocket exploded on its launch pad while it was being examined by officers, engineers, and technicians. Over 100 people were burned to death, but the tragedy went unreported. The Soviet Union was determined that their space program be seen as a series of triumphs, and so the inevitable setbacks and disasters were hidden from the world.

STORIES OF SPACE
In the 1950s, the American fascination with space exploration was expressed in science fiction stories.

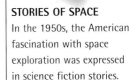

FAMOUS HOUNDS
Belka and Strelka recovered safely from their orbit of the Earth aboard *Sputnik 5*. Strelka later gave birth to six puppies, one of which was given to President Kennedy as a gift from the Soviet Union.

CHAPTER THREE

Space missions

The era of crewed space flight began in 1961 when the Soviet Union put the first man in space. This led to other triumphs, and it seemed as if the United States might lose the battle for technological superiority.

On April 12, 1961, Soviet citizen Senior Lieutenant Yuri Gagarin became the first human being to travel in space and the first to orbit the Earth. This first human space flight cruelly upstaged the American expectations of Project Mercury. It was a highly dangerous experiment, with Gagarin strapped to a seat in a tiny capsule above the booster rocket—much like sitting on top of a giant furnace. Gagarin's departing words at blastoff were "Off we go! Goodbye, see you soon, dear friends." He was carried into space by a modified, more powerful version of the Sputnik launcher, called the Vostok. The craft separated from the rocket on reaching its designated altitude, and then took the cosmonaut once around the Earth. The flight itself lasted just one hour 48 minutes. Nevertheless, it was a journey that no one else had ever made, and the cosmonaut

Yuri Gagarin

Yuri Alexeyevich Gagarin (1934–68) became, in 1961, the first human to travel in space. His early life was humble, but after graduating as a pilot officer, he was selected to train as a cosmonaut at 26. After his groundbreaking space flight, he was raised to the rank of colonel. Tragically, at the age of 34, Gagarin was killed when his fighter plane crashed.

Soviet hero
Although Gagarin made just one space flight, this single achievement made him world-famous. In his own country, he was given the title "Hero of the Soviet Union."

faced unknown problems. No one had ever been in space, and it was not at all certain what the experience might reveal. Were human beings suited for space at all? Might something unthinkable occur when he rode in orbit? Might he go mad, or burst, or suffer unusual symptoms? It is reported, however, that Gagarin remained calm throughout. No doubt his composure was one of the reasons he was chosen for the unique honor of being the first man in space. "I see Earth! I see the clouds! It's beautiful, what beauty!" he commented. He wrote down his thoughts in a school notebook, but eventually his pencil, which was not tied down, floated out of reach. He could have floated, too, but he preferred to keep himself strapped to his seat.

On reentry, the instrument module failed to separate from his capsule, and the

SPACE CAPSULE
Gagarin's tiny snail-like capsule landed in a field near Saratov in the southwestern Soviet Union.

craft began to spin and wobble. Meanwhile, the capsule's outer skin glowed as atmospheric friction heated it by several thousand degrees. Disaster was averted when, after ten minutes, the heat and vibration caused the module to break loose, and his craft steadied its progress. At 23,000 ft (7,000 m) altitude, he was ejected automatically from his seat, and landed safely by parachute in a Russian field, to the alarm of the locals who happened to witness his descent. He had floated down from the sky in an orange pressure suit, and was mistaken for a being from some other planet. Yet he was of the Earth, and he had triumphed. On his return, Gagarin became the most celebrated man of his age. In the Soviet Union, he became a shining image of technological superiority.

Many details of Gagarin's flight were hidden by the Soviet authorities, encouraging a rumor that it had not actually taken place and the Soviets had, instead, fooled the world with an elaborate confidence trick. (The same accusations would be leveled at the US Apollo landing on the Moon some eight years later.) Yet he had done it. There was no denying the scale of the Soviet advance.

An American success was now desperately required. It became imperative for Project Mercury to launch a mission as soon as possible, and the world waited for an American to fly into space. On May 5, 1961, less than one month after Gagarin's mission, astronaut Alan Shepard stepped into a spacecraft called *Freedom 7* and was blasted to a height of 110 miles (180 km). Shepard's flight lasted a little over 15 minutes. His trip was suborbital, his rocket lacking the power to match the pull of gravity, so it was modest compared with Gagarin's full orbital flight. Like Gagarin, Shepard also prevailed. His only problem on the flight seems to have been the

SPLASHDOWN
Astronaut Alan Shepard is lifted out of the ocean onto a US Marine helicopter after his successful suborbital flight on May 5, 1961. Until the space shuttle emerged in the 1980s, all US astronauts returned from space missions by "splashing down" in the ocean.

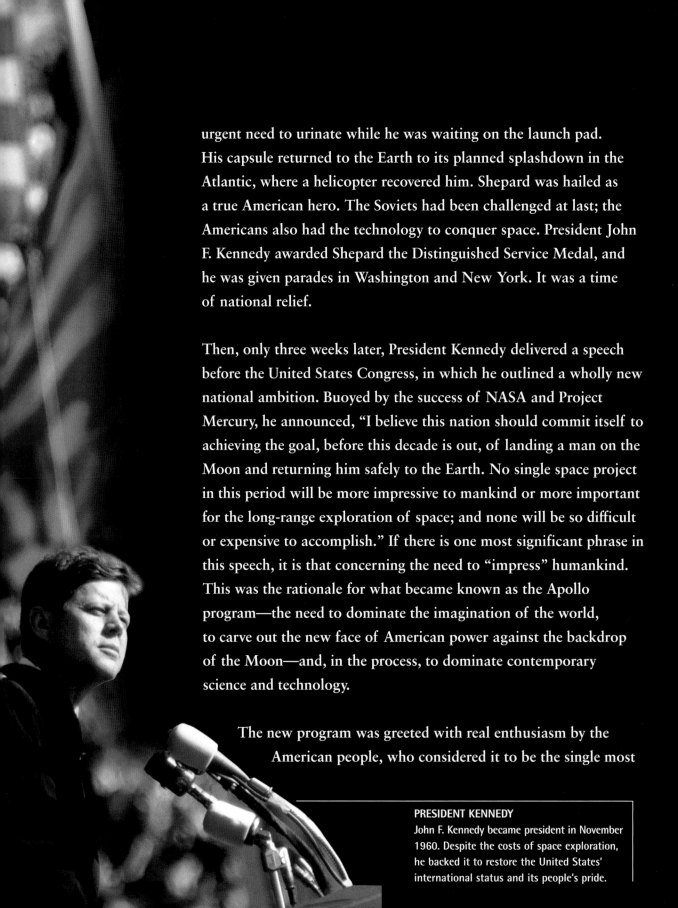

urgent need to urinate while he was waiting on the launch pad. His capsule returned to the Earth to its planned splashdown in the Atlantic, where a helicopter recovered him. Shepard was hailed as a true American hero. The Soviets had been challenged at last; the Americans also had the technology to conquer space. President John F. Kennedy awarded Shepard the Distinguished Service Medal, and he was given parades in Washington and New York. It was a time of national relief.

Then, only three weeks later, President Kennedy delivered a speech before the United States Congress, in which he outlined a wholly new national ambition. Buoyed by the success of NASA and Project Mercury, he announced, "I believe this nation should commit itself to achieving the goal, before this decade is out, of landing a man on the Moon and returning him safely to the Earth. No single space project in this period will be more impressive to mankind or more important for the long-range exploration of space; and none will be so difficult or expensive to accomplish." If there is one most significant phrase in this speech, it is that concerning the need to "impress" humankind. This was the rationale for what became known as the Apollo program—the need to dominate the imagination of the world, to carve out the new face of American power against the backdrop of the Moon—and, in the process, to dominate contemporary science and technology.

The new program was greeted with real enthusiasm by the American people, who considered it to be the single most

PRESIDENT KENNEDY
John F. Kennedy became president in November 1960. Despite the costs of space exploration, he backed it to restore the United States' international status and its people's pride.

obvious token of US supremacy. That enthusiasm was in large part based on a belief in the absolute powers of science. This was considered to be an age of miracles, and there seemed no reason why it would not continue indefinitely. The presence of a young and charismatic president

MERCURY CAPSULE
Grissom squeezes into his Mercury capsule, the *Liberty Bell 7*. Astronauts always sat with their backs against the bottom of the capsule, facing the top.

GRISSOM'S CLOSE CALL
Gus Grissom, along with a medical officer, walks free from the *Liberty Bell* after splashdown difficulties. He nearly drowned when his spacesuit began to fill with water.

helped to lift the mood of the nation further. It was not coincidental that one of the slogans for John F. Kennedy's 1960 presidential campaign was "New Frontiers." The history of the United States was determined by the steady removal of frontiers in the West, as pioneers slowly made their journey across the continent in search of new land. The space frontier was another barrier to be conquered. In the aspiration toward the Moon, Kennedy's slogan could be publicly and triumphantly justified. Kennedy also wished to dominate the superpower politics of the day, and his speech was a direct challenge to the Soviet Union. The Soviets did respond, in conditions of utmost secrecy, by preparing for their own crewed missions to the Moon.

When a second American Mercury astronaut, Gus Grissom, completed another suborbital flight in July 1961, it was marred by an unsatisfactory splashdown in the Atlantic, which almost drowned him and led to the loss of the space capsule. The escape hatch on Grissom's capsule, the *Liberty Bell*, blew off while it was bobbing in the sea. In fear of drowning, Grissom quickly scrambled out into the water. The rescue helicopter was up to its wheels in the water as it tried to recover the *Liberty Bell*, but the capsule sank to the ocean floor.

SPREADING THE NEWS
In the Soviet Union, news of the faultless flight of cosmonaut Gherman Titov was received joyously. Any unsuccessful Soviet missions were kept secret.

Grissom was foundering, too, having forgotten to close the oxygen valve on his spacesuit, which was now filling with water. Grissom survived, but the mission did little to advance the US in the space race.

Sixteen days later, the Soviets countered the faulty American mission with the astonishing flight of Gherman Titov. The cosmonaut stayed in space for a whole day, and orbited the Earth 17 times before making a faultless reentry and a parachute touchdown in a plowed Russian field. His achievement was clear. The 15-minute rides of Shepard or Grissom seemed, in Soviet premier Nikita Krushchev's words, like "a flea's jump" in comparison. Furthermore, like Gagarin, Titov had actually flown over the United States, and in the popular imagination the land of America was under threat from these foreign travelers in outer space. Suddenly the world seemed much smaller. A new term came into being—the space gap. For Americans it meant the uneasy realization that the Soviets had much more powerful rockets. Then, in the fall of that year, 1961, the communists built the Berlin wall, cutting the city in half and confining the citizens of East Berlin to the communist section. The Soviets seemed to be winning the Cold War as well as the space race.

In the increasing scramble for supremacy and publicity, the United States next tried to counteract the effectiveness of Titov's flight with a fully orbital flight by John Glenn. He was launched from Cape Canaveral in February 1962,

BERLIN WALL
At the height of the Cold War, the Soviets built a wall cutting the German city of Berlin in two. It prevented those in communist East Berlin from moving to capitalist West Berlin. In the 28 years the wall stood, 263 people were killed trying to climb it to escape to the West.

SPACEMAN
John Glenn, shown here wearing his *Mercury 7* suit, was one of the first US astronauts.

having been preceded on the launch pad over the previous months by a dummy astronaut and a monkey named Enos, in order to test all the systems in space flight. Glenn orbited the Earth three times in five hours in a flight he described as "smooth and easy." He reported a phenomenon that other astronauts would see on later flights, too. It appeared that a swarm of brilliantly lit fireflies surrounded his capsule. Thousands of dancing flecks of light, now greenish-blue, now white, now red, could be seen swirling around outside his viewport. These would later be identified as dust particles and frozen droplets of water issuing from the cooling system, but at the time it seemed like some unknown fiery magic of space travel. Glenn splashed down in the Atlantic at the end of what was a hazardous reentry into the Earth's atmosphere. There seemed to be a critical fault with the heat shield; if the shield had failed, the craft—and Glenn—would have burned to a cinder on reentry. Luckily, the fault was a false alarm. After landing, Glenn emerged from the space capsule and found himself famous; the first

FRIENDSHIP 7 LIFTOFF
On February 20, 1962, John Glenn, inside Mercury capsule *Friendship 7*, became the first US astronaut to orbit the Earth.

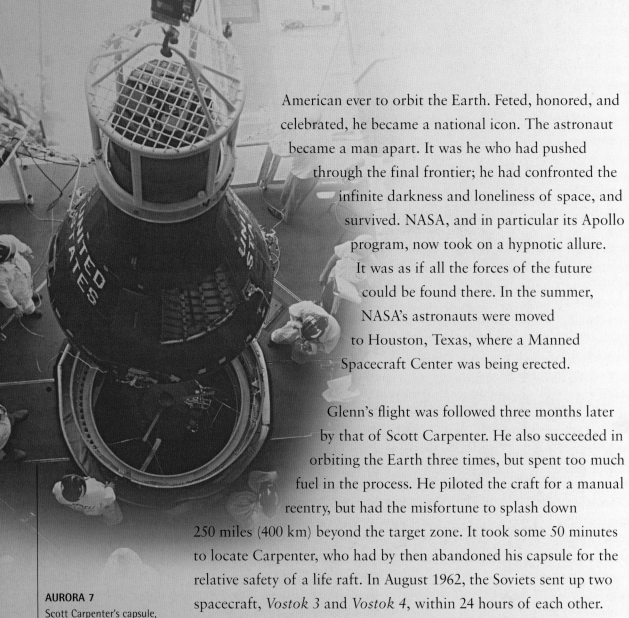

American ever to orbit the Earth. Feted, honored, and celebrated, he became a national icon. The astronaut became a man apart. It was he who had pushed through the final frontier; he had confronted the infinite darkness and loneliness of space, and survived. NASA, and in particular its Apollo program, now took on a hypnotic allure. It was as if all the forces of the future could be found there. In the summer, NASA's astronauts were moved to Houston, Texas, where a Manned Spacecraft Center was being erected.

Glenn's flight was followed three months later by that of Scott Carpenter. He also succeeded in orbiting the Earth three times, but spent too much fuel in the process. He piloted the craft for a manual reentry, but had the misfortune to splash down 250 miles (400 km) beyond the target zone. It took some 50 minutes to locate Carpenter, who had by then abandoned his capsule for the relative safety of a life raft. In August 1962, the Soviets sent up two spacecraft, *Vostok 3* and *Vostok 4*, within 24 hours of each other. In space they flew side by side, as if they were bomber planes on a mission. The US responded to this latest Soviet triumph with Wally Schirra's *Sigma 7* space flight. It threatened another space melodrama, as the launch was almost aborted, but Schirra managed to fly six orbits in what he later described as a "textbook" operation.

There were, however, operations of another, potentially more significant, kind. In the summer of 1962, a satellite known as *Telstar 1*, the most advanced communications device of its kind, was launched. It could transmit television programs across the world,

AURORA 7
Scott Carpenter's capsule, *Aurora 7*, is lowered onto an *Atlas D* launch vehicle, prior to his flight. This was just one of the Project Mercury capsules, which all had the number "seven" appended to them, because they were flown by the first seven astronauts chosen by NASA.

then a spectacular feat. A seven-minute
program was broadcast from France to
the United States, succeeded a few hours
later by the first-ever live images transmitted
from Great Britain to North America. Such
images have now become familiar, of course, but in
1962, the notion of actually seeing events as they took
place thousands of miles away was extraordinary. For the
first time, it was now possible for the peoples of the world to
have an immediate, simultaneous sensory experience. Just 12 days
after *Telstar 1* beamed its first pictures, 16 nations took part in a
diverse television program linking the US and Europe. It was
not a coincidence that two of the Americans involved in these
proceedings were John Glenn and Wally Schirra. The astronauts
were the masters of ceremonies of this new technological civilization,
the ambassadors of the future.

PRIVATE TELEVISION
Telstar, the first satellite
to send TV signals
around the world, was
also the first satellite to
be developed and built
for commercial profit.

If there was going to be a future, that is. In the fall of 1962, the
United States and the Soviet Union confronted each other in earnest

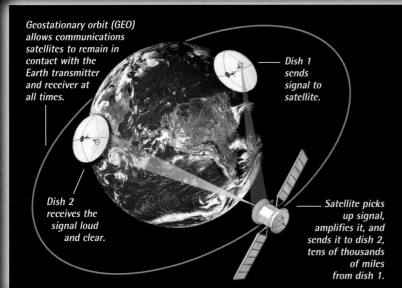

Geostationary orbit (GEO)
allows communications
satellites to remain in
contact with the
Earth transmitter
and receiver at
all times.

Dish 1
sends
signal to
satellite.

Dish 2
receives the
signal loud
and clear.

Satellite picks
up signal,
amplifies it, and
sends it to dish 2,
tens of thousands
of miles
from dish 1.

Different types of satellites

Many human-made satellites orbit the
Earth. Some communicate telephone
and TV signals by bouncing them from
one side of the world to another.
Others, known as Global Positioning
System (GPS) satellites, aid navigation.
Some even plot weather patterns and
monitor pollution. Satellites have
different orbits depending on their
role, but most types of satellites travel
in geostationary orbit (GEO), meaning
that they orbit the Earth in the same
direction and at the same speed as
the Earth rotates, so they appear
to be stationary above a fixed point.

rather than through the shadow-boxing of the space race. Two years earlier, Soviet premier Nikita Khrushchev had promised to protect the island of Cuba, a Caribbean outpost of communism. Khrushchev had a nuclear missile base secretly installed on the island, only 90 miles from the US mainland. The Soviet missile site could not be concealed indefinitely and, on October 15, 1962, President Kennedy was shown photographs, taken by two high-flying reconnaissance aircraft, of the missile bases on Cuban soil. It was estimated that medium-range nuclear missiles could destroy the defenses of the United States in just 17 minutes. Kennedy had to act quickly and forcibly. "The greatest danger of all," he said, "is to do nothing." He placed the US army on alert, and thousands of air force reserves were called up. He debated with his colleagues the option of invading Cuba, but it was feared that the Soviets might then invade West Berlin. An air strike on the missile site was

NUCLEAR FEAR
In the 1960s, the tension of the Cold War between the United States and the Soviet Union increased. Both sides developed more and more nuclear weapons, as well as better rocket technology that could deliver them anywhere in the world.

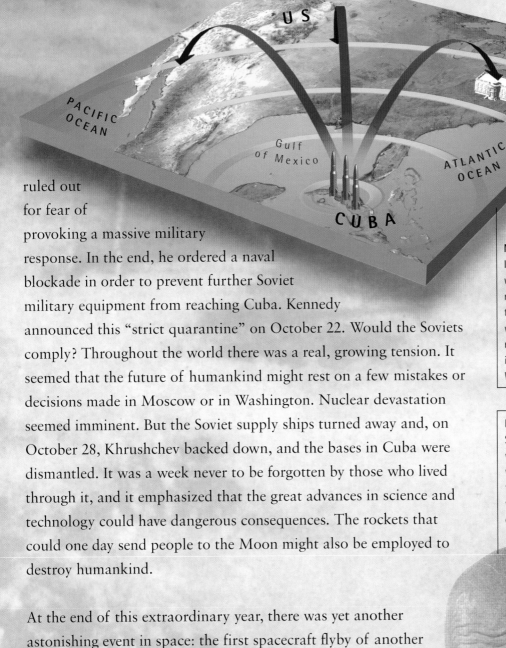

US

WASHINGTON
DC

PACIFIC
OCEAN

Gulf
of Mexico

ATLANTIC
OCEAN

CUBA

ruled out
for fear of
provoking a massive military
response. In the end, he ordered a naval
blockade in order to prevent further Soviet
military equipment from reaching Cuba. Kennedy
announced this "strict quarantine" on October 22. Would the Soviets
comply? Throughout the world there was a real, growing tension. It
seemed that the future of humankind might rest on a few mistakes or
decisions made in Moscow or in Washington. Nuclear devastation
seemed imminent. But the Soviet supply ships turned away and, on
October 28, Khrushchev backed down, and the bases in Cuba were
dismantled. It was a week never to be forgotten by those who lived
through it, and it emphasized that the great advances in science and
technology could have dangerous consequences. The rockets that
could one day send people to the Moon might also be employed to
destroy humankind.

MISSILES IN CUBA
In 1962, the Soviet Union
was installing medium-
range nuclear missiles on
the island of Cuba. These
were capable of reaching
many parts of the US,
including the capital,
Washington, DC.

DANGEROUS GAMBLE
Soviet premier Khrushchev
wrongly thought the US
would back down before
the Soviet Union. But it
was his country that finally
conceded to US demands.

At the end of this extraordinary year, there was yet another
astonishing event in space: the first spacecraft flyby of another
planet. On August 27, 1962, the US had launched *Mariner 2*
on a path toward Venus, the second planet from the Sun.
Mariner 2 looked rather like a hexagonal drum,

with antennae and a pair of solar panels (for charging its battery) standing up like wings. This winged messenger sped through the vacuum of space at about 2.5 miles (4 km) per second. *Mariner 2* flew by its destination less than four months later. To this day it still orbits the Sun. NASA scientists had packed the craft with sensors rather than cameras, which could not have penetrated the planet's cloud layers. These sensors determined that an atmosphere of carbon dioxide enveloped the planet and trapped the Sun's heat, making the surface of Venus blisteringly hot. This was a planet out of Hell.

This first successful planetary mission astounded scientists. Some had believed that steamy swamps might lie beneath the clouds, while others had suspected oceans of near-boiling water. *Mariner 2* overturned their general perception that Venus would somehow be a lovely, if lifeless, planet. It also suggested to scientists that the other planets in our Solar System might be as alien and uninhabitable as Venus.

VENUS FLYBY

The first space probe to fly by another planet was *Mariner 2*. Launched on August 27, 1962, on December 14 that year it came within 21,000 miles (34,000 km) of Venus, and was able to transmit details of the planet's atmosphere back to Earth.

VOLCANIC VENUS

The highest volcano on Venus, Maat Mons, is 5 miles (8 km) high and about 250 miles (400 km) across. Probably inactive, it towers over a lifeless desert of solidified lava.

ВЕНЕРА-9 22.10.1975   ОБРАБОТКА ИППИ АН СССР 28.2.1976

PICTURES OF ANOTHER WORLD

In 1975, *Venera 9* transmitted the first photographs of the Venusian surface. They showed a landscape of jagged rocks that stretched into the distance before being swallowed up in the dense atmosphere.

After *Mariner 2*'s flyby, further missions to Venus transmitted data back to Earth. Between 1961 and 1983, the Soviet Union launched a series of space probes, under the name Venera, which were designed to enter the atmosphere of Venus and actually land on the surface. Many of them were destroyed before returning data, or after just a short period of operating. But in 1970, *Venera 7* touched down on Venus, becoming the first space probe ever to land successfully on another planet. The first-ever photographs of the Venusian surface were transmitted by *Venera 9* in October 1975. Later probes, delivered by American as well as Soviet spacecraft, disclosed a forbidding world of volcanoes both living and dead. The surface itself has been transformed by volcanic activity, with lava flows solidified into great plains of stone. One such flow measures almost 1,000 miles (1,610 km) across. There are dunes created by the Venusian wind. There are volcanic plateaus in the shape of

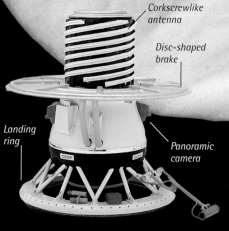

Exploring Venus

Although Venus has a few similarities with Earth—it is about the same size, and is surrounded by a substantial atmosphere—the planet the Venera probes encountered is a hostile place indeed. Its cloud layer is nearly 18.5 miles (30 km) deep. The atmosphere is almost entirely composed of carbon dioxide and is so thick that nothing more than half a mile (800 m) away could possibly be seen. The atmospheric pressure is 90 times that of the Earth—capable of crushing a human within seconds. Raging winds blow deadly sulfuric acid clouds around the whole planet every four days. The temperature is 840°F (450°C), hot enough to melt lead. This is a scorching, poisonous, unfriendly world.

Corkscrewlike antenna

Disc-shaped brake

Landing ring

Panoramic camera

Venera 9
The lander *Venera 9* touched down on Venus on October 22, 1975 and became the first probe to send back pictures from the surface of another planet.

pancakes, steep at the sides and flat on top. There is the faintest possibility of life floating somewhere within the sulfuric acid clouds, for they contain water droplets, too. What form that life might take is beyond anyone's present estimation.

This Venusian adventure could hardly have been contemplated even 10 years earlier. Spacecraft had been designed to operate in temperatures greater than 840°F (450°C), at an atmospheric pressure 90 times that of the Earth, and fitted with scientific instruments that could transmit information across many millions of miles of space. To the general public, these technological feats seemed extraordinary, and they confirmed that science itself was still the greatest forum of human achievement.

In May 1963, a few months after *Mariner 2*'s epic journey to Venus, NASA continued its crewed missions around our own blue planet. Astronaut Gordon Cooper remained in space for 34 hours, completing 22 orbits of the Earth. Cooper was so relaxed in the minutes leading up to his launch that he actually fell asleep in the capsule. One of the medical

GORDON COOPER'S FAITH 7
The Mercury-Atlas rocket launched Gordon Cooper in *Faith 7* from Cape Canaveral, Florida. After this mission, NASA's Project Mercury was abandoned in favor of the more ambitious Project Gemini.

experiments assigned to him involved the collection of his own urine for analysis back on Earth, to help find out how weightlessness affected the human body. He was provided with a syringe to transfer the liquid from a receptacle to a special container, but the syringe leaked. The unfortunate Cooper spent much of the mission surrounded by a drifting swarm of golden droplets. Cooper's lengthy stay in space was a triumph for Project Mercury, which came to an end with his return to Earth. For the public, however, the novelty of the astronaut adventure was beginning to diminish.

In the following month, the Soviet Union countered Cooper's flight by sending the first woman into space. The cloak of secrecy that surrounded any Soviet mission prevented Valentina Tereshkova from telling even her mother about the mission, and she concocted a story about special parachute training. Tereshkova was launched in *Vostok 6* and, in 71 hours, made 48 orbits of the Earth, despite suffering from severe space-sickness. Her mother was reportedly furious when she discovered the truth. Beyond her own front door, though, Tereshkova became a heroine. It would be another two decades before the United States sent a woman into space.

Human space flight had now become a known quantity. The Soviet Union and the United States seemed evenly matched both in space technology and in the skills and endurance of their cosmonauts and astronauts. The plans of the space agencies in both countries were now turning to the infinitely more dangerous and complex journey to come—that of reaching the Moon itself.

ASTRONAUT'S-EYE VIEW
Astronaut Gordon Cooper had extraordinarily acute eyesight, and during his long flight he reported being able to see roads, rivers, and the smokestack of a steam train in the cloudless Himalayas.

WOMAN IN SPACE
On June 16, 1963, Valentina Tereshkova became the first woman to travel in space. Following her flight, she became a role model for women all over the world.

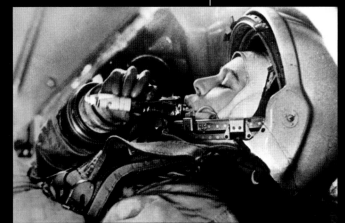

CHAPTER FOUR

America *takes the* lead

With the successful completion of Project Mercury, NASA turned its attention to a new series of missions called Project Gemini. Their aim was to test spacecraft and prepare astronauts for a crewed landing on the Moon.

The assassination of President Kennedy on November 22, 1963 had deeply shocked Americans. In his honor, the Launch Operations Center at Cape Canaveral was renamed the Kennedy Space Center, and the new president, Lyndon B. Johnson, vowed to continue with Kennedy's challenge to put a man on the Moon. As a necessary first step, NASA was sending a series of uncrewed spacecraft, called Ranger, to the Moon. The Rangers were designed to crash-land on the Moon's surface after transmitting TV images of their approach. The first successful one was *Ranger 7* which, in July 1964, managed to transmit more than 4,000 images of the Moon's surface. The *Ranger's* six cameras showed the pitted and cratered landscape in extraordinary detail. But this was only the beginning of the lunar journey. In what was now becoming

a familiar pattern, the Soviet leadership decided to go one stage further than the Americans. Project Gemini was about to launch two-man flights, and so the premier of the Soviet Union, Nikita Khrushchev, decreed that his nation—his empire—would send up three men. Hence was born the Voskhod venture. It was a striking example of how politics dictated the uses to which technology was put. The politicians, not the scientists, were the masters. Space exploration was an extension of their power.

Vladimir Komarov, Boris Yegorov, and Konstantin Feoktistov duly entered their capsule in October 1964, in conditions of extreme discomfort and even danger. There was no room for ejection seats, so there was no possibility of escape in the event of a launch failure. They could hardly move within the cabin, since they were lying side by side. It was, for them, a mercifully short flight of 24 hours. Nevertheless, it was hailed as a further triumph of Soviet technology.

The aura of prestige surrounding the Soviet Union was heightened when, in the spring of 1965, a cosmonaut performed the first spacewalk (known as extravehicular activity or EVA). Alexei Leonov stepped into space from the airlock of *Voskhod 2*, and spent some 12 minutes gyrating before the television cameras for an amazed world. It was a truly heroic feat to float above the Earth—to have only a protective suit between you and infinite space—to have the whole globe of the Earth as your companion. All this was a cause for wonder. There was one unforeseen development in this strange scenario. Leonov's suit expanded in the vacuum of space, to the point where he could not return through the airlock. He struggled for eight minutes—a harrowing scene the cameras, unsurprisingly, did not record. Eventually, almost exhausted by his efforts, Leonov reduced his suit's air pressure in order to squeeze through the port, and he nd his commander returned in the craft to the safety of Russian forests and snow. It was later revealed that Leonov had carried a suicide pill in his helmet in case of an absolute emergency.

The Americans duly applauded the feat and then went back to their own work with even greater determination and urgency. There were no fewer than six Gemini missions in 1965, five of them crewed. In June, Edward White became the first American to walk in space. He was outside *Gemini 4* for 21 minutes, tethered by a gold-plated umbilical cord that conducted oxygen, power and communications. To maneuver, White fired a gas gun. He and James McDivitt went on to complete a record four-day mission, but it was beaten two months later by *Gemini 5*. Gordon Cooper and Peter Conrad stayed in orbit for eight days on board *Gemini 5*. At the end of the year, there was yet more evidence of rapidly growing technological expertise. *Gemini 6* and *Gemini 7* were launched from Cape Canaveral within 11 days and approached within 12 in (30 cm) of each other in space. It was an extraordinary accomplishment by the pilots. The US had always celebrated its technological achievements, but the skills of US astronauts were now also applauded. Those skills were tested even further by astronauts

STEP INTO SPACE
During the first US spacewalk, on June 3, 1965, Ed White tested a special hand-held unit, which allowed him to propel himself while performing maneuvers in space.

Luna spacecraft

Between 1959 and 1972, the Soviets had 20 successful Moon missions with several lunar "firsts." These included: first probe to impact the Moon, first flyby and image of the far side of the Moon, first soft landing, first lunar orbiter, and first analysis of lunar soil.

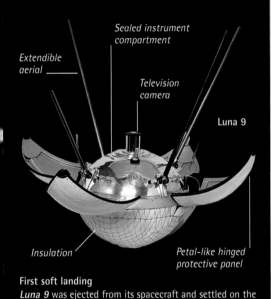

Extendible aerial

Sealed instrument compartment

Television camera

Luna 9

Insulation

Petal-like hinged protective panel

First soft landing
Luna 9 was ejected from its spacecraft and settled on the Moon's surface. There, petal-like panels opened up to reveal scientific apparatus and a television camera system.

Borman and Lovell in *Gemini 7*, who stayed in space for two weeks. It was the longest time ever recorded for a space mission and, significantly, represented the maximum length of time that NASA expected a Moon mission might take.

The US was showing its prowess in all areas of space exploration. In the middle of the Gemini program, for example, the first commercial communications satellite, *Early Bird*, was successfully launched. But then the Soviets once again managed to pull off a surprising achievement in the face of American supremacy. In February 1966, a craft known as *Luna 9* performed the remarkable feat of landing undamaged on the surface of the Moon. As the spacecraft approached, a rocket was fired downward to slow its descent. With just 16 ft (5 m) to go, a capsule emerged, rolled onto the lunar surface, righted itself, and then unfolded the panels of its casing to expose a television camera. The camera completed a panoramic survey of the immediate area, which, unsurprisingly enough, revealed a flat expanse with some rocks and boulders in the distance. But once more it was a revelation. Here was a distant landscape, utterly hostile to human life; yet we could examine it in detail. It was almost as if we

could

see into Heaven

or Hell and investigate

their surroundings. Two months later,
Luna 10 went into orbit around the Moon, the first
spacecraft ever to do so. In June, an American craft, *Surveyor 1*, also
accomplished a soft landing on the lunar surface. Further Surveyor
spacecraft soft-landed on the Moon until the end of 1967, as another
stage in the larger US program to send the first humans to the Moon.
These spacecraft demonstrated the feasibility of a crewed landing
and identified possible landing sites.

RENDEZVOUS IN SPACE
This photograph, taken by
a *Gemini 7* crew member,
shows *Gemini 6* in orbit.
The two spacecraft carried
out the first rendezvous in
space in December 1965.

Project Gemini was entering its most productive phase. The main
purpose of the final five missions was to test various docking
procedures in space, as well as to lengthen the time of the spacewalks
and the duration of the missions themselves. On March 16, 1966, Neil
Armstrong and David Scott, in *Gemini 8*, attempted the first docking
in space by linking up to an Agena rocket. But there was a problem.
When coupled together, the vehicles began to roll. The pilots tried
firing thrusters in order to stabilize the crafts, and then even
undocked from the Agena. Nothing seemed to work. Their roll
accelerated to such an extent that they were spinning at one
revolution per second. "We have serious problems here," Scott

Panoramic view
of the Moon

ANGRY ALLIGATOR
Gemini 9 ran into trouble when the protective cover on the docking adapter failed to open properly—the crew described it as the "angry alligator."

SPLASHDOWN
The *Gemini 8* capsule returned to Earth in an emergency splashdown area in the Pacific Ocean, just 3 miles (4.8 km) from the recovery ship.

reported to launch control. "We're rolling up and can't turn anything off." It was only when Armstrong fired the thrusters for reentry, burning up precious fuel, that the rolling ceased. An electrical short-circuit was later identified as the cause of *Gemini 8*'s close brush with disaster. Three months later, another technical fault prevented *Gemini 9* from docking, and it was not until July 18, 1966 that *Gemini 10* performed the first wholly successful docking, again with an Agena rocket. *Gemini 11* and *Gemini 12* followed approximately the same program of activities, culminating in a mission lasting four days and a spacewalk of more than two hours.

By 1967, some 400,000 Americans were working on the Apollo program. There were just three years left to fulfill Kennedy's challenge to land a man on the Moon before 1970, and the first Apollo flight was planned for February 1967. Inevitably, there were casualties in such an intensive and dangerous pursuit. In January 1967, astronauts

Gus Grissom, Roger Chaffee, and Edward White were taking part in a training session in the cabin of *Apollo 1* when a spark ignited some equipment in the cabin and set the atmosphere of pure oxygen alight. Sixteen seconds later, there was an explosion, and the three men died of suffocation. The Apollo program was delayed for two years while a more reliable capsule was designed. It seems likely that, in the haste of the space race, certain safety procedures had been neglected. Space races could be deadly.

Three months after the conflagration on *Apollo 1*, cosmonaut Vladimir Komarov was killed testing the latest Soviet spacecraft, the *Soyuz* (see p. 77). From the beginning of the flight he encountered severe problems. Yet as a result of superb piloting, he managed to fly the *Soyuz* manually back into the Earth's atmosphere, without any electronic backup. But the spinning craft became entangled with the parachute supposed to bear him safely back to Earth: Komarov and *Soyuz* hit the ground at a speed of 300 miles (480 km) per hour. He gained the melancholy distinction of being the first human being to die after returning from space. The Soyuz program, like the Apollo, was then thoroughly revised and overhauled. Yet it now had to function without its founding father, Sergei Korolev, who had died the previous year. While the Apollo command modules were being investigated in the

APOLLO DISASTER
This is the command module of *Apollo 1* after the fateful fire. There was such intense heat and smoke after the explosion that it took the rescue team 5 minutes to get the hatch open.

APOLLO CREW
Although it never got off the ground, the mission in which Gus Grissom (right), Ed White (center), and Roger Chaffee (far right) perished was given the name *Apollo 1*.

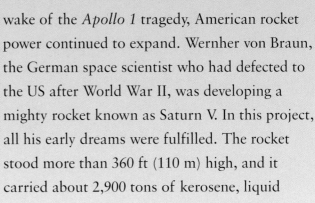

TESTING THE SATURN
The Saturn V rocket's second test launch occurred on April 4, 1968, at the Kennedy Space Center. This uncrewed test flight identified a number of problems that had to be solved before a crew could fly on the rocket.

wake of the *Apollo 1* tragedy, American rocket power continued to expand. Wernher von Braun, the German space scientist who had defected to the US after World War II, was developing a mighty rocket known as Saturn V. In this project, all his early dreams were fulfilled. The rocket stood more than 360 ft (110 m) high, and it carried about 2,900 tons of kerosene, liquid oxygen, and liquid hydrogen in its thin metal skin. Saturn V was the mightiest vehicle in the world, and it was going to the Moon. In November 1967, the world witnessed Saturn V's first, uncrewed test launch. Its thrust at liftoff was equivalent to 180 million horsepower, and there was the sound and sensation of an earthquake for miles around the launch pad.

The Soviets were aware of these developments, of course. Throughout 1967 and 1968 they were engaged in a series of preparatory tests for their lunar program. Since 1962, they had been designing a rocket that could bear comparison with

MIGHTY SATURN V
Everything to do with this rocket is huge. Here, the first flight stage of the rocket leaves the vehicle assembly building for the stage test building at the Michoud Assembly Facility near New Orleans in 1968.

Saturn V, called the N1. It was also intended to send two men to the Moon. However, repeated technical faults delayed test launches. The first launch, in 1969, was terminated by a ruptured oxygen pipe. Three further tests, up to 1972, all ended in disaster. On each occasion the rocket exploded, causing enormous damage to Baikonur Cosmodrome and the surrounding area. The N1 would never make a successful flight.

This series of failures effectively brought to an end the Soviet ambition to beat the Americans to the Moon. It might have been that the absence of Sergei Korolev had some part in the steadily declining abilities of the Soviet space program. They certainly had little to show for a determined effort to beat the United States, involving the expenditure of billions upon billions of rubles (equivalent to roughly half the costs of Apollo). Yet it had all begun so well, and so successfully, with the flights of Gagarin and Titov.

Saturn V rocket

Made up of three stages, each with a unique role to perform, the Saturn V was the only rocket capable of lifting the huge mass of fuel needed to travel to the Moon and back.

STAGE THREE

The final stage has a restartable engine that puts it into orbit, then reignites to send it to the Moon.

Second stage falls away.

Launch escape tower is jettisoned.

STAGE TWO

The second stage engine is ignited and takes the rocket toward the 24,855 mph (40,000 km/h) needed to escape the Earth's gravitational pull.

Once the kerosene fuel and liquid oxygen are consumed, the empty first stage falls back to Earth.

STAGE ONE

The first stage lifts the vehicle into the high atmosphere. The five F-1 engines consume 15 tons of fuel per second at launch.

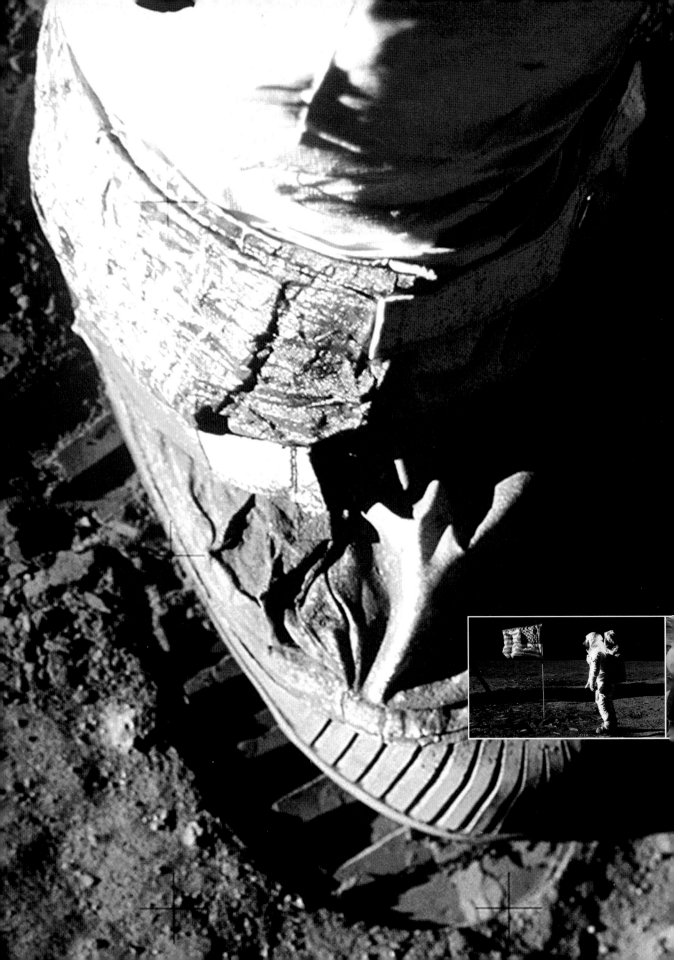

CHAPTER FIVE

One *small* step...

As the Apollo program recorded success after success, lunar fever began to infect the world. By 1968, it became clear that NASA was indeed planning to fulfill President Kennedy's promise to land a man on the Moon before 1970.

As if to underline its new supremacy in space, the United States launched the first crewed Apollo flight, *Apollo 7*, in October 1968. Then, on December 21, *Apollo 8* was launched from the newly erected Moonport at Kennedy Space Center. *Apollo 8*'s three astronauts, Frank Borman, James Lovell, and William Anders, were the first humans to journey to the Moon. They completed 10 lunar orbits in a little over 20 hours, and transmitted live television pictures of the lunar surface. For the first time, the Earth itself was photographed from space. Jim Lovell described the planet as "a grand oasis in the big vastness of space." In March 1969, the lunar module was taken up by *Apollo 9* and tested in space. This was the module that would take the astronauts down to the surface of the Moon and then boost them back into space. The module

Foot restraints, known as "golden slippers," on the porch where the astronaut stood during extravehicular (EVA) activity.

LUNAR MODULE
Apollo 9 was the first crewed flight to include the lunar module (LM). This view shows the LM in its lunar-landing configuration.

was known as "the spider" because of its appearance. It was composed of two parts, one for descent and landing (with a hatch and a ladder so that the astronauts could clamber down to the surface) and one for ascent and reunion with the mother ship. The test flight of *Apollo 9* was successful and, on May 18, *Apollo 10* was launched. The crew's mission was to conduct all the phases of Apollo spacecraft operations, including rendezvous and docking in lunar orbit, except the actual lunar landing. Nothing could be left to chance in what was, in any case, a highly dangerous exercise.

For many people, the success of the Apollo missions was the forerunner of much greater ambitions. It was, of course, necessary that an American should soon land upon the Moon in order to demonstrate the technological prowess of the United States, but those first steps were intended to be followed by others. It seemed plausible that, in a very few years, human beings would be able to construct and inhabit colonies upon the lunar surface. Science fiction had long predicted such colonies, in the form of cocoons or bubbles, and the rapid escalation of technical progress suggested that these fantasies could soon become realities. So the Apollo missions were watched with great interest not just by fellow astronauts and scientists but by the ordinary citizens of the United States, and of the world.

On July 16, 1969, *Apollo 11* was launched. Neil Armstrong, Edwin "Buzz" Aldrin, and Michael Collins climbed into their Apollo spacecraft above a Saturn V rocket. As they lay side by side, they ran through the sequence for which they had been trained so meticulously. They were above the biggest engines in the history of the world. The propellant was piped into the tanks, and the flight program loaded into the computers. Beneath their command module was the service module; beneath that, the lunar module itself, christened the *Eagle*, which would separate and touch down on the surface of the Moon.

Before being transported to the launch pad, the astronauts' helmet visors had been lowered and a stream of oxygen piped into their suits. Ten seconds before liftoff, a million gallons of water were sprayed onto the launch pad to absorb the acoustic shock of the firing, and prevent damage to the launch pad, the rocket, and its payload. Four seconds later, the first-stage engines were ignited and the vehicle seemed to explode with 180 million horsepower of thrust. The rocket punched through the layers of cloud in its irresistible journey upward. After a flight of 12 minutes, the rocket reached orbital velocity—17,500 mph (28,000 km/h). Then, as one astronaut put it, "It's like this giant hand grabs the orbiter and throws it into space."

READY TO GO
Neil Armstrong, followed by Buzz Aldrin and Michael Collins, make their way to the transfer van that would take them the 8 miles (13 km) to Launch Pad 39A.

The astronauts lay in silence—literally an unearthly silence after the roar of the engines and the blast of the rocket. After 2 hours 44 minutes, Neil Armstrong switched on the third-stage rocket that boosted them from the Earth's orbit. That stage was then jettisoned, and the journey to the Moon began.

Light takes about one and a half seconds to cross 238,350 miles (384,400 km), the distance to the Moon. *Apollo 11* did it in three days. On the third day, when they were about 70 miles (112 km) above the Moon's surface, Neil Armstrong and Buzz Aldrin descended into the lunar module and stood side by side, held to the floor by elastic restraint cords, at the control panel. The lunar module separated from the command and service modules, which remained linked as a single unit under the sole command of Michael Collins. From two triangular windows, Armstrong and Aldrin watched as what Buzz Aldrin called the "magnificent desolation" of the Moon came closer and closer. But the descent took longer than anticipated, and the crew overshot their planned destination. They were heading straight for a crater, the rocky surface of which might damage the craft and

PREFLIGHT PRACTICE
During missions, astronauts needed to complete many tasks while weightless. Here, Neil Armstrong practices in a lunar module (LM) simulator prior to the actual mission.

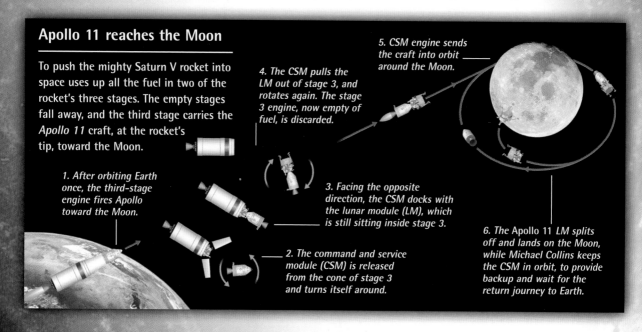

Apollo 11 reaches the Moon

To push the mighty Saturn V rocket into space uses up all the fuel in two of the rocket's three stages. The empty stages fall away, and the third stage carries the *Apollo 11* craft, at the rocket's tip, toward the Moon.

1. After orbiting Earth once, the third–stage engine fires Apollo toward the Moon.

2. The command and service module (CSM) is released from the cone of stage 3 and turns itself around.

3. Facing the opposite direction, the CSM docks with the lunar module (LM), which is still sitting inside stage 3.

4. The CSM pulls the LM out of stage 3, and rotates again. The stage 3 engine, now empty of fuel, is discarded.

5. CSM engine sends the craft into orbit around the Moon.

6. The Apollo 11 LM splits off and lands on the Moon, while Michael Collins keeps the CSM in orbit, to provide backup and wait for the return journey to Earth.

APOLLO 11 LIFTOFF

On July 16, 1969, the
Kennedy Space Center
in Florida was filled
with a mighty roar. The
huge Saturn V rocket, with
engines blazing, launched
Apollo 11 toward the Moon.
At the tip of the rocket
is the white command
module, which sits on top
of the gray service module.

could remain in the Moon's dust for millions of years.

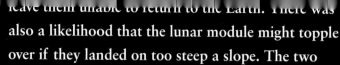

leave them unable to return to the Earth. There was also a likelihood that the lunar module might topple over if they landed on too steep a slope. The two astronauts prepared for disaster. But whatever fate, or divinity, looks after human exploration then extended its protection. Neil Armstrong, his heart racing at 160 beats per minute, took over manual control of the craft and managed to maneuver the *Eagle* to a safe landing point. The spacecraft touched down on the lunar surface unscathed, the four green lights of its landing stage winking in the capsule. Armstrong transmitted back to Earth the words, "Houston,

LUNAR LANDSCAPE
The Moon's desolate, cratered surface as it would have appeared to the astronauts during their final approach in the lunar module.

Tranquillity Base here. The *Eagle* has landed." It is no exaggeration to state that the people of the world watched and wept.

Armstrong broadcast his first perceptions—the first of the human race—from the surface of this alien and deserted world. "The area out of the left-hand window is a relatively level plain with a fairly large number of craters of the five- to 50-foot variety… and literally thousands of little, one- and two-foot craters around the area… it's pretty much without color, it's gray." The innumerable craters described by Armstrong are the result of meteorite impacts, many of them dating back four billion years. The Moon's flat plains, or "seas," are the product of lava flows from deep fractures in the crust.

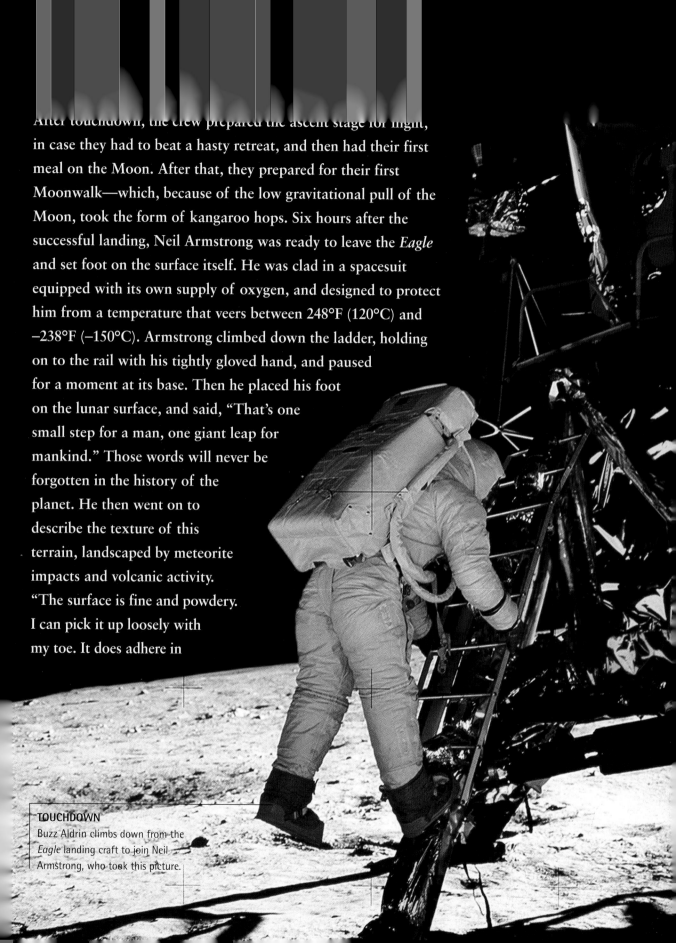

After touchdown, the crew prepared the ascent stage for flight, in case they had to beat a hasty retreat, and then had their first meal on the Moon. After that, they prepared for their first Moonwalk—which, because of the low gravitational pull of the Moon, took the form of kangaroo hops. Six hours after the successful landing, Neil Armstrong was ready to leave the *Eagle* and set foot on the surface itself. He was clad in a spacesuit equipped with its own supply of oxygen, and designed to protect him from a temperature that veers between 248°F (120°C) and −238°F (−150°C). Armstrong climbed down the ladder, holding on to the rail with his tightly gloved hand, and paused for a moment at its base. Then he placed his foot on the lunar surface, and said, "That's one small step for a man, one giant leap for mankind." Those words will never be forgotten in the history of the planet. He then went on to describe the texture of this terrain, landscaped by meteorite impacts and volcanic activity. "The surface is fine and powdery. I can pick it up loosely with my toe. It does adhere in

TOUCHDOWN
Buzz Aldrin climbs down from the *Eagle* landing craft to join Neil Armstrong, who took this picture.

fine layers, like powdered charcoal, to the soles and sides of my boots... I can see the footprints of my boots and the treads in the fine, sandy particles." Those footprints will still be there, and the traces of human life left on the surface may be preserved for many millions of years, undisturbed by wind or rain.

The return to Earth

The lunar module (LM) blasts off the Moon's surface and docks with the orbiting command and service module (CSM). The command module (CM) then splits off and returns the astronauts to Earth.

2. Astronauts transfer from LM to CSM, and the LM splits off. CSM fires its engine to return to Earth.

1. LM splits in two; the lower half remains on the Moon and acts as a launch pad for the top half, which blasts off to join the orbiting CSM.

3. As the CSM approaches Earth, the service module (SM) is jettisoned, leaving just the CM, with the three astronauts inside.

4. Heat shield protects the CM as it descends through the Earth's atmosphere. Parachutes open and the CM splashes down in the Pacific Ocean.

Simplified diagram, not to scale.

Aldrin joined Armstrong on the surface, and together they began the range of scientific experiments assigned to them. They set up a system of reflectors designed to calculate the distance from the Earth to the Moon precisely, and established a seismograph to measure Moon tremors.

The astronauts unveiled a plaque that read: "Here men from the planet Earth first set foot upon the Moon. July 1969 AD. We came in peace for all mankind." They planted an American flag upon the lunar surface, an important gesture for their country. They had some difficulty in anchoring it securely in the lunar dust, but eventually fixed it in an upright position, where it remains to this day. For the Soviets, it was to be a permanent reminder that their opponents had finally beaten them in this race to the Moon. Armstrong and Aldrin remained in front of the flag for a televised interview with President Richard Nixon, who congratulated them from the White House in what he described as "the most

A SPECIAL FLAG
NASA designed a flagpole with a horizontal bar that allowed the flag to "fly" without the help of any wind.

LUNAR EXPERIMENTS
During their stay, the astronauts carried out scientific experiments. Below, they are shown testing for seismic activity and solar wind.

historic telephone call ever made." Above them, the two astronauts could see the blue globe of the Earth itself, a bright and iridescent world compared to that on which they stood. They collected together samples of lunar rock and dust and then, after only 2 hours 31 minutes of exploration, returned to the lunar module, so covered with Moon dust that Armstrong remarked that they looked like chimney sweeps.

Only 22 hours after the landing, it was time to prepare for an awkward and possibly hazardous ascent. Aldrin activated the ignition and, to the two astronauts' relief, the module began its climb back to the command and service module (CSM) piloted by Michael Collins. After the lunar module reached orbit, the CSM was able to approach and gently dock. Michael Collins remembered thinking, "We really are going to carry this off!" The three astronauts began their return to Earth. They required one mid-course correction in order to

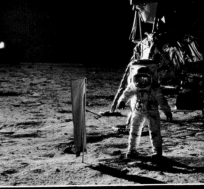

complete their journey successfully, and bad weather made it necessary to move the splashdown point in the Pacific Ocean by some 215 miles (346 km). There was no backup to assist them in the case of an emergency, so each subtle change of plan was fraught with risk. But no insurmountable problems arose, and they splashed down successfully in the Pacific after a mission that had lasted eight days.

SPLASHDOWN AND AWAY
The command module (CM), with the flotation collar that prevented it from sinking, is hoisted away. The outer shield of the craft was designed to burn off during reentry.

IN QUARANTINE
On the recovery ship *Hornet*, President Richard Nixon congratulated the three astronauts through the window of their mobile quarantine facility.

A decade of planning, and a thousand years of speculation, had come to fruition. The great adventure was over and the plaudits were immense. On their return, the astronauts were placed in quarantine for 16 days and examined by doctors, in case they had become infected with strange alien germs. When the three were judged to be unharmed, they were released to a jubilant public. Armstrong, Aldrin, and Collins were heroes almost everywhere in the world. On a 38-day tour, they visited 23 countries. In the major American cities, they were welcomed with ticker-tape parades. Among many congratulations from world leaders were these words from New Zealand's prime minister Keith Holyoake: "The impossible is only that which takes a little longer to do."

HORNET + 3

The world had watched in awe. Two television cameras, one mounted on the *Eagle* and another set up on the lunar surface, had fed images to the world's televisions. Some 600 million people, about one-fifth of the Earth's population, watched Armstrong and Aldrin walking on the Moon. Public screens had been erected in the world's major cities. Where there were no televisions, people had pressed their ears eagerly to radios, or read of the landing in newspapers. President Nixon's pronouncement that "for one priceless moment in the whole history of Man, the people of this Earth are truly one" was barely an exaggeration.

There was no such enthusiasm in the Soviet Union. In fact, the Soviets had tried to rival the American success by landing a robot probe, *Luna 15*, on the Moon at precisely the time when Armstrong and Aldrin were on its surface. The probe failed during its descent, crashing into the Moon's aptly named Sea of Crises. After the triumph of *Apollo 11*, however, the Soviet Union declared that it had never been involved in a race to land men on the Moon. Secretly, though, they continued to develop their lunar program, with the hope of one day sending men to the Moon, until the project was finally scrapped in 1974.

VICTORY PARADE
New Yorkers showered the *Apollo 11* astronauts in ticker tape as they paraded down Broadway and Park Avenue.

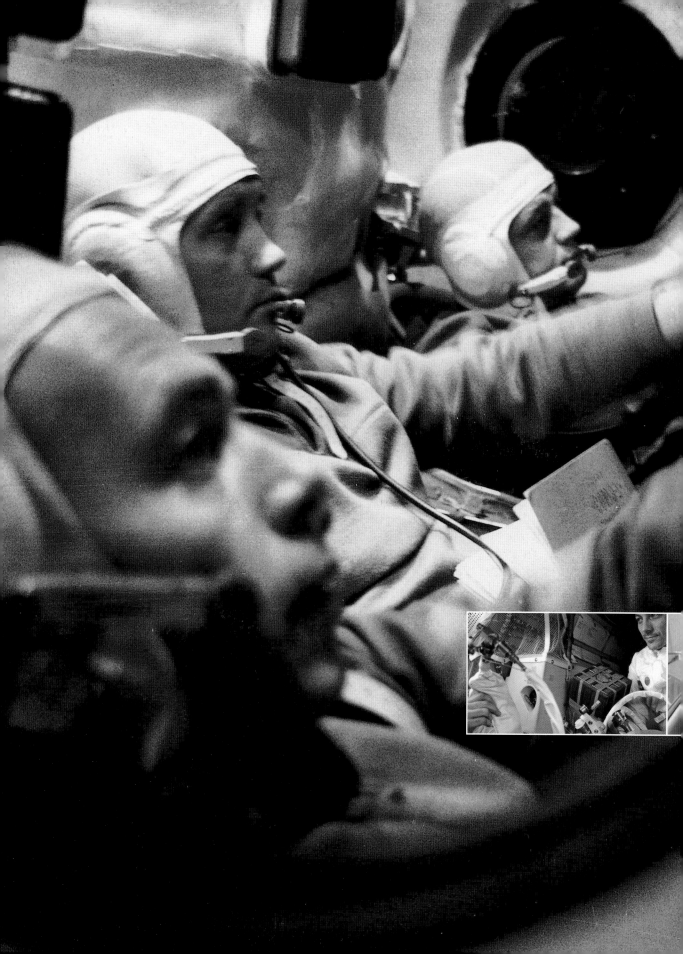

CHAPTER SIX

Trouble *in* space

There were to be six further Apollo missions, although none would enjoy the sheer thrill of the first manned landing. But with the launch of Apollo 13 on April 11, 1970, a new kind of drama in space was about to unfold.

Just six months after *Apollo 11*, *Apollo 12* was on the same journey. This time the astronauts traveling to the Moon were Pete Conrad, Alan Bean, and Richard Gordon. Conrad landed the lunar module, the *Intrepid*, just 200 yd (186 m) from *Surveyor 3*, an unmanned probe NASA had sent up in 1967 to sample the surface. It was as if they were parking a car. Part of their task was to recover the camera and other parts of the *Surveyor* spacecraft, which was located just to the south of the Ocean of Storms. Conrad

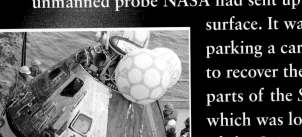

and Bean performed two moonwalks, during which they collected samples of rock, dust, and small beads of natural glass, which they found everywhere on the lunar surface. They also studied the composition of the solar wind, a stream of charged particles that flows from the Sun. The crew spent over 30 hours on the lunar surface. The mission was successful, yet although it was longer and more complex than its predecessor, it generated only a fraction of its interest. In one sense, that was predictable; the first journey is always more intensely interesting, since it is a journey into the unknown. But it also reflects the capacity of the public mind to lose its curiosity and excitement about the most extraordinary events, and rapidly to become indifferent to the achievements of science and technology. The feat, once it has been performed, is taken for granted. Almost as soon as Neil Armstrong and his colleagues had returned to the Earth, the idea of men on the Moon had become familiar and routine.

Public interest, however, was revived by the dramatic *Apollo 13* mission in the spring of the following year. Astronauts James Lovell, Jack Swigert, and Fred Haise took off from the Kennedy Space Center on April 11, 1970, on a journey planned to take them to the side of a lunar crater known as Fra Mauro. The engines caused some problems soon after launch, but the malfunction was soon rectified.

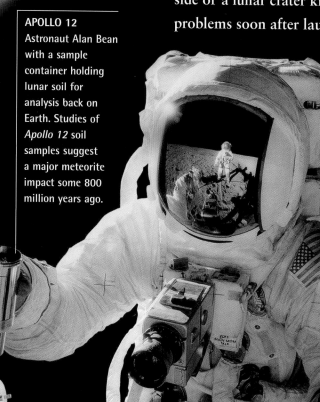

APOLLO 12
Astronaut Alan Bean with a sample container holding lunar soil for analysis back on Earth. Studies of *Apollo 12* soil samples suggest a major meteorite impact some 800 million years ago.

The mission seemed to be on course. After leaving Earth orbit, *Apollo 13* shot across space, gradually slowing down as the planet's gravity tried to pull it back. But then, two days into the flight, when they were some 200,000 miles (322,000 km) out in space, the astronauts heard an explosion. Swigert, strapped into his seat, also sensed a vibration. There was a master alarm, used to warn the crew of a major systems problem or failure, and a sudden loss of power. At this point Jack Swigert transmitted a message to NASA, "Hey, we've got a

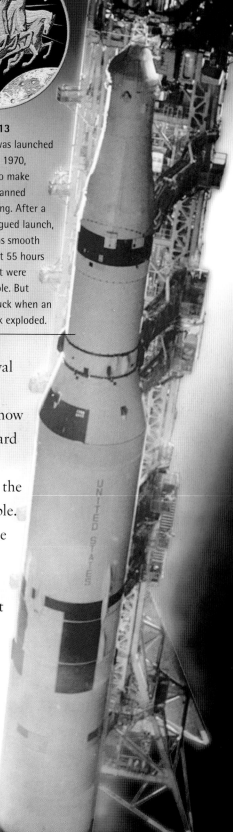

problem here." There was indeed a problem. A liquid oxygen tank had exploded in the service module, discharging its contents and effectively disabling the module. A great cloud of liquid oxygen floated away from them into deep space; with it went their main source of the life-giving gas and the Apollo spacecraft's ability to generate power. The three men were alone in space, drifting in a wreck. They had been trained not to panic in an emergency, but their lives were in imminent and overwhelming danger. There was a real possibility that they would be lost in space, helpless until they became asphyxiated.

UNLUCKY 13
Apollo 13 was launched on April 11, 1970, intending to make the third manned Moon landing. After a trouble-plagued launch, progress was smooth and the first 55 hours of the flight were unremarkable. But disaster struck when an oxygen tank exploded.

It quickly became apparent that the only possibility of survival lay with the lunar module, *Aquarius*. It would have to be employed as a rescue craft to bring them back to Earth. But how would they achieve this unparalleled feat while speeding toward the Moon? It was necessary first to start up the power of the lunar module, before shutting down the command system of the service module, in order to conserve as much power as possible. Now all oxygen and power came from *Aquarius*. It was of the utmost importance that the crew were returned to Earth as quickly as possible, since the lunar module was equipped to support just two men for less than 50 hours. On the best available evidence, it would

BLOWN OXYGEN TANK
Apollo 13 lost its main source of power when one of its oxygen tanks exploded. The switches that controlled the tank's temperature had welded shut. The temperature should have remained below 80°F (27°C), but it soared to 1,000°F (538°C).

now have to support three men for the next 84 hours. There was only one course available to them—the free return. This was a planned trajectory that would send the spacecraft around the Moon, whose gravity would pull the craft to a greater speed, before a well-timed engine burn fired the craft out of the Moon's orbit and back to Earth. This "slingshot" maneuver was hazardous, given the condition of the craft, but there was no alternative.

The operation was successful, but it had hardly been accomplished before another serious problem occurred. The crew realized that levels of carbon dioxide in the craft were rising sharply—there was a major problem with the air-renewal system. The lunar module did not have enough filter canisters to continue removing the carbon dioxide breathed out by the crew. Although the command module contained a supply of canisters, these did not fit the lunar module's air-cleaning system. In imminent danger of suffocation, James Lovell and Jack Swigert managed, with the aid of NASA engineers talking through the procedure with them,

LUNAR LIFEBOAT
When *Apollo 13*'s service module was disabled, the crew used the LM, *Aquarius*, as a rescue craft.

MISSION CONTROL
Four teams at mission control worked around the clock in order to give constant advice to the *Apollo 13* crew.

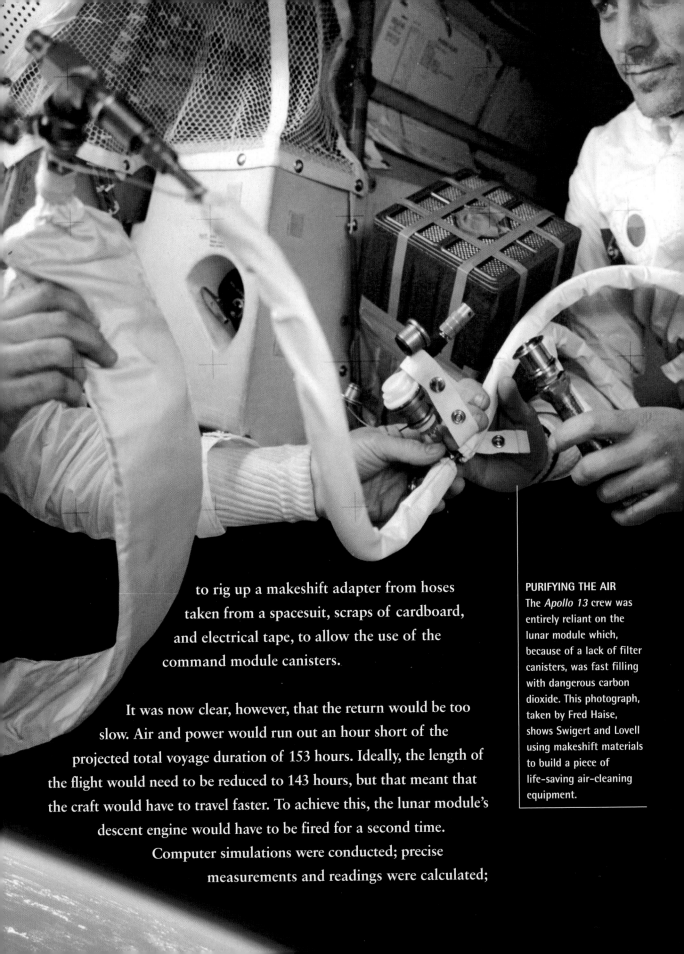

to rig up a makeshift adapter from hoses
taken from a spacesuit, scraps of cardboard,
and electrical tape, to allow the use of the
command module canisters.

It was now clear, however, that the return would be too
slow. Air and power would run out an hour short of the
projected total voyage duration of 153 hours. Ideally, the length of
the flight would need to be reduced to 143 hours, but that meant that
the craft would have to travel faster. To achieve this, the lunar module's
descent engine would have to be fired for a second time.
Computer simulations were conducted; precise
measurements and readings were calculated;

PURIFYING THE AIR

The *Apollo 13* crew was
entirely reliant on the
lunar module which,
because of a lack of filter
canisters, was fast filling
with dangerous carbon
dioxide. This photograph,
taken by Fred Haise,
shows Swigert and Lovell
using makeshift materials
to build a piece of
life-saving air-cleaning
equipment.

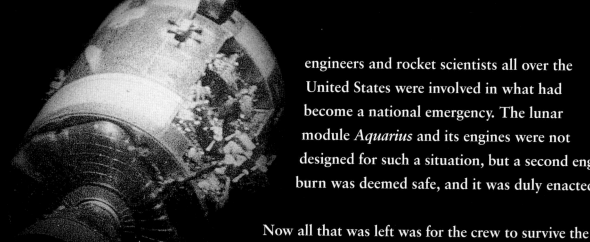

engineers and rocket scientists all over the United States were involved in what had become a national emergency. The lunar module *Aquarius* and its engines were not designed for such a situation, but a second engine burn was deemed safe, and it was duly enacted.

Now all that was left was for the crew to survive the cold, damp, cramped conditions for another 62 hours. Water was dripping from the cabin walls, the temperature had plummeted to 37.4°F (3°C) and the computer system was on the verge of collapse. Yet the lunar module was so sturdy, and its engines so reliable, that the craft remained on its predetermined course. Then, six and a half hours before their reentry into the Earth's atmosphere, it was confirmed that the batteries did not have enough power to retain all the functions of the command module. Without vital power, the crew would be dead before reaching Earth. It was agreed that the batteries would be fully employed only at the last possible moment—just two and a half hours before reentry. As James Lovell put it later, "We had a dead service module, a command module that had no power, a lunar module ... that didn't have a heat shield." And they were soon to descend toward the surface of their planet at an enormous, crushing speed.

Four and a half hours before reentry, the astronauts maneuvered the craft to a suitable angle and jettisoned the service module, which fell back into space with all its glittering debris. Three hours later, the lunar module, their robust lifeboat, was discarded and fell back to Earth. Mission control on Earth transmitted the message, "Farewell, *Aquarius*, and we thank you." Now the three men were in the command module, plummeting back to Earth. They began to feel the pressure of gravity on them but, after their ordeal, the

DAMAGED MODULE
As *Apollo 13* neared Earth, the service module was jettisoned. As they watched it drift away, the astronauts saw that one of its panels was blown off.

GRIM CONDITIONS
Inside the cramped lunar module, the temperature dropped to 38°F (3°C), and the portholes were covered with frost. Sleep was almost impossible for the three *Apollo 13* astronauts.

sensation must have seemed welcoming. They splashed down in the Pacific Ocean, within three miles of the rescue carrier *Iwo Jima*. They had survived. The successful return was greeted with relief all over the world. In the United States, churches had remained open throughout the ordeal, and even the stock exchange had paused for a moment of prayer. President Nixon, awarding the three the Presidential Medal of Freedom, commented, "The three astronauts did not reach the Moon, but they reached the hearts of millions of people." More importantly for the space program, *Apollo 13* had proved the durability of the space hardware and the ingenuity of all involved in the successful rescue mission.

Less than a year later, *Apollo 14* was launched to complete its predecessor's unfinished business.

HOME AT LAST
The cold, exhausted *Apollo 13* astronauts were picked up by the recovery ship *Iwo Jima* after splashdown in the Pacific (below).

The first American in space, Alan Shepard, was among the crew, which touched down on the Moon on February 5, 1971, in precisely the area that had been earmarked for *Apollo 13*. Astronauts Shepard and Edgar Mitchell remained on the surface for one and a half days. A modular equipment transporter—a sort of lunar wheelbarrow—allowed them to collect weighty samples of lunar rock.

APOLLO 14
Astronaut Alan Shepard shades his eyes as he looks across the Moon's sunlit surface. Shepard and Mitchell spent a record 9 hours 24 minutes on the lunar surface.

Since the late 1960s, both the United States and the Soviet Union had been pondering the concept of a space station permanently circling the Earth. It could be used as a launch pad for further space exploration and as a platform for scientific experiments and observations. Three months after the launch of *Apollo 14*, the Soviets launched the world's first space station—*Salyut 1*, the first stage of an ancient human dream, to create a city in the sky. This first space station was, however, just 50 ft (15.5 m) in length. In its cramped interior were storage lockers for food and water, exercise equipment for the cosmonauts, and even a miniature greenhouse so that plant growth in zero gravity could be observed. It was planned that the cosmonauts would spend up to a month in space. At one end of the craft was a docking module. Here a space ferry, known as Soyuz, could be attached, to bring and return the cosmonauts on their tours of duty. Yet immediately there were problems. *Soyuz 10* failed to dock successfully, and its mission was aborted. Six weeks later, after 24 hours of exhausting maneuvers, *Soyuz 11* managed to dock with *Salyut 1* and, on June 7, 1971, three cosmonauts entered the space station. The three men engaged in a series of scientific tests, many of which concerned their own reactions and responses. No one had ever dwelled in space for so long, and biological readings were required.

After 23 days aboard the space station, the longest time any humans had survived in space, the three cosmonauts

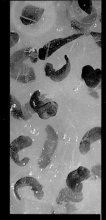

SPACE FROGS
On *Salyut 1*, the cosmonauts hatched tadpoles to find out if zero gravity affected their development.

left *Salyut 1* and returned to the *Soyuz 11*. They undocked, and began their short return to Earth. They were about to reenter the Earth's atmosphere when something happened. There was an accident. A valve in the spacecraft, which equalized the pressure inside and outside the *Soyuz* cabin, had opened in space. Within one minute the cabin had depressurized and the cosmonauts were dead.

Soyuz 11 landed in the Soviet Union under automatic control, and the bodies of the crew were found by a rescue team sent out to search for the stricken ship. At once the Soviet authorities canceled the next Soyuz mission. In future missions, cosmonauts would wear spacesuits on reentry, which would save their lives in the event of an involuntary depressurization. But the requirements of these bulky suits forced a redesign of the Soyuz craft, which took an entire year. Meanwhile, the *Salyut 1*, out of use, was sent back down through the atmosphere to burn up. It had not had a happy history.

ILL-FATED CREW
The three-cosmonaut crew of the world's first space station, *Salyut 1*, died when their *Soyuz* capsule malfunctioned while returning to Earth.

The Soyuz space ferry

The Soyuz (from the Russian for "union") spacecraft was conceived by Sergei Korolev's design bureau in the early 1960s, as part of the Soviet lunar program. Unlike the earlier Vostok, the Soyuz could conduct active maneuvering, orbital rendezvous, and docking. In spite of two serious accidents, the Soyuz has gone on to become the longest-serving manned spacecraft in the world, operating since 1967. In 1975, it performed the historic docking with an Apollo spacecraft. It has been used to transport cosmonauts and paying customers to the International Space Station.

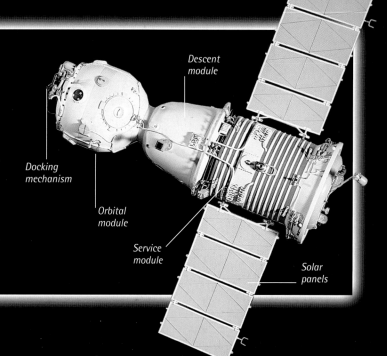

Descent module

Docking mechanism

Orbital module

Service module

Solar panels

CHAPTER SEVEN

Beyond *the* Moon

The Soyuz 11 tragedy had served only to highlight American supremacy in space. The last Apollo missions continued without mishaps, and NASA's attentions then turned to adventures beyond our Moon—exploring the planets in our Solar System.

On July 26, 1971, *Apollo 15* was boosted toward the Moon on the now-familiar Saturn V rocket. While previous Apollo missions had chosen the great plains of the lunar surface for their landing sites, *Apollo 15* had quite a different target. It touched down on the rocky and mountainous terrain of the Hadley-Apennine region. The Apennines are the largest mountain range on the Moon; Mount Hadley itself rises just under 3 miles (4.5 km) above the surface. The astronauts' task was to obtain samples of soil and rock over as wide an area as possible. To achieve this, they used a battery-operated, four-wheeled buggy known as a lunar rover, which could move over the difficult terrain at a speed of about 6 miles (9.6 km) per hour. They gathered valuable geological evidence, including the Genesis Rock, a greenish lump that would later be dated at about four billion years old—almost as old as the Moon itself. Over three days, the two astronauts spent a total of 19 hours exploring the Moon, covering a distance of about 18 miles (29 km). No human beings had ever traveled farther on the Moon. And what a journey theirs was. They observed vast canyons and endless valleys, impossibly high mountains and great chasms. Because of the closeness of the horizon and the absence of familiar features, the astronauts could not calculate the scale of the hills and mountains around them. It was a landscape out of a dream or nightmare; truly an alien world.

On April 20, 1972, *Apollo 16* touched down in a highland region known as Descartes, in

Examining lunar rocks

Between 1969 and 1972, the Apollo astronauts gathered a total of 842 lb (382 kg) of Moon rock and soil samples. In 1969, the Lunar Receiving Laboratory was built at the Johnson Space Center in Texas to preserve and analyze these specimens.

Breccia lunar rocks
Meteorites hit the Moon's surface, smash apart, and heat and shatter the surrounding rocks. The jagged, melted mixture of fragments then stick together and harden to form rocks known as breccias.

Hot gases leave bubble-shaped holes in the cooled lava.

Basalt lunar rocks
The dark areas of the Moon are called seas, or maria, but are in fact made up of dark rock known as basalt. This rock is cooled, hardened lava that, more than three billion years ago, seeped out from deep beneath the Moon's surface and oozed over low-lying areas.

Polished basalt, seen through a microscope.

What had become, for watchers on the Earth, a routine landing on the Moon. For the first time, the astronauts used a special ultraviolet camera to take images of gas clouds and galaxies. *Apollo 17*, the final mission, was launched at midnight on December 7, 1972, and four days later, it landed among the steep valleys and ancient mountains by the edge of the Sea of Serenity. Among other samples, the crew collected a specimen of mysterious orange soil, found to be glass beads created in an ancient volcanic eruption.

No one has gone back to the Moon. The commander of the *Apollo 17* mission, Eugene Cernan, became, on December 14, 1972, the last of 12 men ever to have walked on its surface. At the birth of the new millennium, three of these 12 were dead and the others entering old age. Far from the hundreds of

EXPLORING THE MOON
Here, Harrison Schmitt of *Apollo 17*, the only trained geologist to walk on the Moon, collects lunar samples from the mountainous Taurus-Littrow region. Of all the Apollo missions, *Apollo 17* explored more of the Moon's surface and collected the greatest quantity of lunar rock.

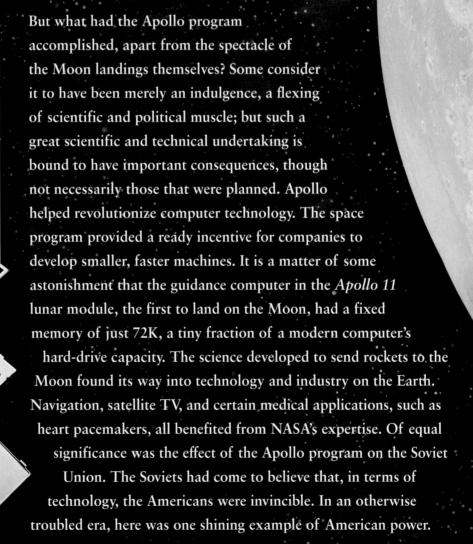

lunar travelers that were once predicted, there will come a time when there is no one still living who has walked on the Moon's surface. Debate continues about the possibility of setting up crewed stations on the Moon, or staging posts from which to mount further space voyages, or platforms for observing the stars. By 1972, however, as far as American ambition and public opinion were concerned, the Moon had been "done."

COMPUTER TECHNOLOGY
The computer in *Apollo 11*'s lunar module had just 72K of memory. Since 1969, technological advances have made computers smaller and more powerful. Today, even some graphic calculators can store over 500K of information.

But what had the Apollo program accomplished, apart from the spectacle of the Moon landings themselves? Some consider it to have been merely an indulgence, a flexing of scientific and political muscle; but such a great scientific and technical undertaking is bound to have important consequences, though not necessarily those that were planned. Apollo helped revolutionize computer technology. The space program provided a ready incentive for companies to develop smaller, faster machines. It is a matter of some astonishment that the guidance computer in the *Apollo 11* lunar module, the first to land on the Moon, had a fixed memory of just 72K, a tiny fraction of a modern computer's hard-drive capacity. The science developed to send rockets to the Moon found its way into technology and industry on the Earth. Navigation, satellite TV, and certain medical applications, such as heart pacemakers, all benefited from NASA's expertise. Of equal significance was the effect of the Apollo program on the Soviet Union. The Soviets had come to believe that, in terms of technology, the Americans were invincible. In an otherwise troubled era, here was one shining example of American power.

Even as the
Apollo
astronauts sat in
their buggy, rolling up hills and down craters,
a craft known as *Mariner 9* was journeying
toward Mars. The probe represented the latest stage
in a NASA program that had been quietly running
since before the emergence of the Apollo program—
the quest for life on Mars.

Mars is the planet that most resembles our own. It is our neighbor in
the Solar System (at its closest approach it is some 35 million miles,
or 56 million km, from the Earth); it has seasons, polar ice caps,
and a 25-hour day. For hundreds of years, Mars has fascinated
astronomers. In the late 18th century, dark areas detected on
its surface were believed to be seas. A century later, an Italian
astronomer, Giovanni Schiaparelli, claimed to see straight lines across
the planet. He called them *canali*—meaning "channels." Many
people interpreted his word literally and believed these to be canals
built by some form of intelligent life. Speculation reached new heights
with the publication of British author H. G. Wells's 1898 novel *The
War of the Worlds*, in which Martian invaders devastate Earth.

MARINER 4
After a seven-and-a-half-
month journey, *Mariner 4*
finally flew past Mars. It
gave scientists their first
glimpse of the Martian
world by sending back
pictures of about one
percent of the surface.

The first successful probes that had visited Mars were in the
American Mariner series. On November 28, 1964, *Mariner 4* had
been launched, on an Atlas rocket, to fly by Mars and take images
of its surface in the hope of capturing some evidence of life. It took
22 photographs, revealing a wasteland of craters and sand. Most
importantly, it discovered that the atmospheric pressure is
less than one percent of that of the Earth—about the
same as it is 18.5 miles (30 km) above the
Earth's surface. This was much

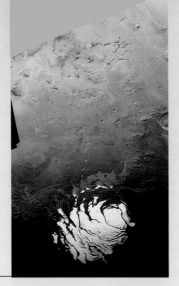

DRY ICE ON MARS
The south pole of Mars is covered by an ice cap of frozen carbon dioxide ("dry ice") that measures roughly 250 miles (400 km) across.

lower than many experts had predicted, and it made the possibility of finding life there remote. Of the canals there was no sign; these would later be dismissed as an optical illusion.

When it arrived at its destination in November 1971, *Mariner 9* became the first artificial satellite of Mars. Its purpose was to gain more information about the atmosphere and the surface of the planet. On its arrival, however, that surface was obscured by giant dust storms, which raged for about two months. So the orbiter circled and waited. When the dust settled, *Mariner 9* began its work.

Mariner 9 orbited the planet for 349 days, taking more than 7,000 images. They showed a frozen world, with sheets of ice and frozen deserts of dunes and craters. Vast canyons—greater than any of those on the Earth—and great volcanic mountains were revealed. The largest volcano on Mars, Olympus Mons, was found to be 17 miles (27 km) high and 435 miles (700 km) across. It is three times higher than Earth's highest feature, Mount Everest, and it is, in fact, the largest known volcano in the entire Solar System. *Mariner 9* discovered that there are plains in the north and highlands in the south, which have been bombarded by millions of meteorites over billions of years. Carbon dioxide makes up the planet's atmosphere, and in winter the poles are covered with carbon dioxide ice.

MARTIAN TERRAIN
The surface of Mars is a barren wasteland of red rocks and sand. Its color is due to the planet's iron oxide, or rust, content.

Mariner 9 also detected dry channels resembling river valleys in certain areas, which suggested to the waiting scientists that water—and perhaps living organisms—had once existed here.

The Mariner series was just the beginning of Martian exploration. In 1975, the United States launched two Viking spacecraft to the planet. Their mission was to discover evidence of life. Each craft carried an orbiter and a lander with television cameras. The landers also had equipment for carrying out experiments to search for life. After a journey of some 11 months, both of them successfully entered the planet's orbit and sent down their landing modules. The *Viking 2* lander touched down far to the north of its sister lander, in an area known as Utopia Planitia. In a climate that produced temperatures of−184°F (−120°C), the lander managed to send its signals for over three years. In a warmer climate, the *Viking 1* lander continued transmitting information for almost six years.

The *Viking*'s cameras transmitted extraordinary pictures of

OLYMPUS MONS
The largest volcano in the Solar System is Olympus Mons on Mars. It is 17 miles (27 km) high, but about the size of Arizona, so it has a very shallow slope.

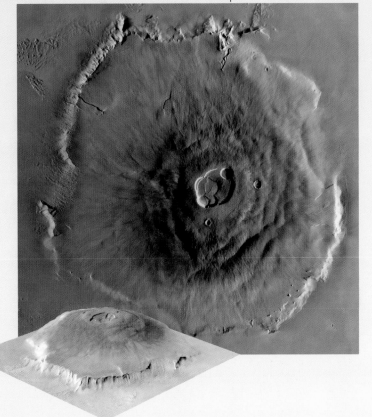

BLUE SUNSETS ON MARS
On Earth, our sky is blue
and our sunsets red, but
on Mars, it is the other
way around. Swirling dust
in the Martian atmosphere
absorbs blue light, leaving
the sky red-orange. At
sunset, this dust scatters
blue light into the area
around the Sun.

GREAT RED SPOT
Jupiter's most famous
feature is the Great
Red Spot (see center of
page)—a fierce hurricane
16,000 miles (25,000 km)
across. It is 5 miles (8 km)
higher than the
surrounding clouds.
Its color comes from
chemicals that form only
high in the atmosphere.

the Martian world. White carbon dioxide frost fell from a pink sky. Rocks and boulders stretched across an orange plain far into the distance. The dust in the atmosphere was sometimes so thick that the Sun was obscured and the rocks cast no shadows—all then became an indistinct orange mist. At other times, wild dust storms swept across the surface.

Under almost daily instructions from controllers on Earth, the landers conducted experiments to find out whether life had been, or still was, possible in this inhospitable environment. One experiment involved cooking the soil to see if any gases with traces of organic (carbon-containing) life were released. In another, nutrients were fed into the Martian soil to see if bacteria would feed on them. There was no response. In spite of the existence of dry river channels, no evidence for life on Mars could be found. Another 20 years would pass before further probes visited the barren red surface.

Running alongside the Martian missions was a series of probes sent to explore Jupiter, the fifth planet out from the Sun and the largest in the Solar System. Jupiter is not a rocky planet, like Mars or Earth, but a gas giant—a vast ball of gas and liquid, of hydrogen and helium, with a tiny inner core of rock. In the spring of 1972, the space probe *Pioneer 10* was launched on a mission to fly by Jupiter. Reaching speeds of over 31,000 miles (50,000 km) per hour, it journeyed for some 21 months before approaching Jupiter's cloud tops. *Pioneer 10* then began to transmit images of the giant planet. It also gathered data on the planet's radiation belts and magnetic field, and discovered that Jupiter is mostly liquid. *Pioneer 10* then flew on beyond the Solar System, continuing to send back valuable data until it finally ran out of transmitting power on February 7, 2003. Subsequent interplanetary probes have extended and deepened our picture of Jupiter. *Pioneer 11* was launched in 1973 to fly by Jupiter and Saturn and on into outer space. It obtained spectacular pictures of Jupiter's Great Red Spot, a hurricane more than twice the size of the Earth, which has raged within the planet's atmosphere for over 300 years. Its sheer size is probably the cause of its long life. Winds on Jupiter's surface reach speeds of 420 miles (600 km) per hour—twice as fast as any hurricane on Earth.

In 1977, two space probes called Voyager were launched: *Voyager 1* to Jupiter, Saturn, and Titan (one of Saturn's moons), and *Voyager 2* on what NASA described as its "grand tour." The configuration of Jupiter, Saturn, Neptune, and Uranus was so aligned that *Voyager 2* would be able to fly past all of them; this would not happen again for another 200 years. Between them, the *Voyagers* transmitted 33,000 images of their first stop, Jupiter. These show clouds that seem to be engaged in perpetual storm, as well as vast areas of swirling gases. Jupiter's surface rotates very quickly, whipping up turbulent clouds of ammonia ice, ammonium sulfide, and water ice. The probes revealed that Jupiter's winds extended over much more of the planet than had been previously supposed; they also recorded flickering northern lights over the polar regions and massive lightning bolts immediately above the clouds. The two *Voyagers* then continued on toward Saturn, which they were to reach in 1980 and 1981.

STORMY JUPITER
This gas giant is 11 times greater in diameter than Earth. Colorful bands of clouds continually sweep around the planet. These clouds rotate at different speeds from one another, causing vortices that turn into violent storms.

PIONEERING PROBE
Pioneer 10, launched in 1972, was designed to conduct the first flyby of Jupiter, and then continue into deep space. In June 1983, it became the first spacecraft to travel beyond the outermost planet of the Solar System.

CHAPTER EIGHT

Space
stations

Although the race to the Moon was over, the space race was not finished yet. Now, the USSR and the US competed to establish a permanent space station in orbit around the Earth, where astronauts or cosmonauts would live and work in space.

During the early 1970s, the Soviets pursued their own attempts at lunar missions. In November 1970, they had landed the first robotic explorer, *Lunokhod 1*, on the Moon. This eight-wheeled vehicle, controlled from the Earth, worked on the lunar surface for 10 months, taking images and testing the surface. The Soviets were also continuing with their space station program, which had started so disastrously with *Salyut 1*. NASA's next grand enterprise was the space shuttle. This was to be a reusable spacecraft

functioning as a space taxi, capable of carrying cargo and passengers into orbit and returning to Earth. Budget cutbacks were to delay the project for several years, however. Meanwhile, the US continued to send probes to other planets during the early 1970s. Seven months after *Pioneer 11* had set out for Jupiter and Saturn,

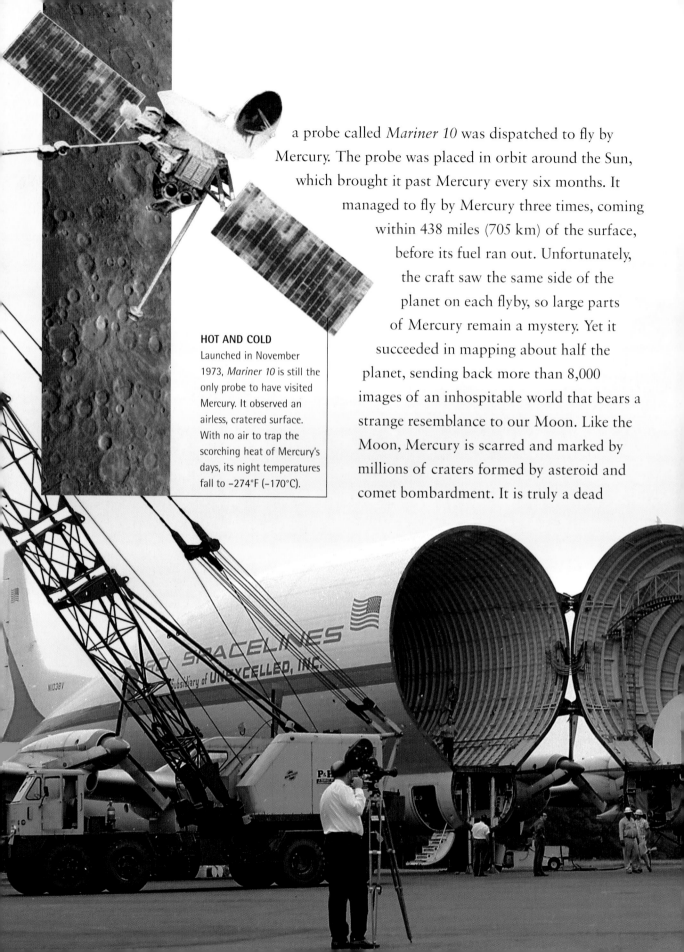

a probe called *Mariner 10* was dispatched to fly by Mercury. The probe was placed in orbit around the Sun, which brought it past Mercury every six months. It managed to fly by Mercury three times, coming within 438 miles (705 km) of the surface, before its fuel ran out. Unfortunately, the craft saw the same side of the planet on each flyby, so large parts of Mercury remain a mystery. Yet it succeeded in mapping about half the planet, sending back more than 8,000 images of an inhospitable world that bears a strange resemblance to our Moon. Like the Moon, Mercury is scarred and marked by millions of craters formed by asteroid and comet bombardment. It is truly a dead

HOT AND COLD
Launched in November 1973, *Mariner 10* is still the only probe to have visited Mercury. It observed an airless, cratered surface. With no air to trap the scorching heat of Mercury's days, its night temperatures fall to −274°F (−170°C).

world. *Mariner 10* no longer functions, but will continue in its solar orbit until it finally disintegrates.

For both space superpowers, 1973 was an eventful year in space station development. In April, the Soviets launched the first units of their next Earth-orbiting space station, *Salyut 2*. When assembled, the station's three units would contain living quarters, a work area, instruments, and a docking mechanism (a port to which visiting spacecraft could attach). Once more, however, technical failures struck the project; *Salyut 2* tumbled out of control and broke apart, and then fell back through the Earth's atmosphere, where it burned up. In the following month, the US was more successful. It launched *Skylab*, its first orbiting space station. *Skylab* was essentially the third stage of a Saturn V rocket, converted into a laboratory and living quarters divided into separate

SKYLAB ASSEMBLY
The first US space station, *Skylab*, was converted from the third stage of a Saturn V rocket. In this photograph, an early test version of *Skylab*, inside a stage of a Saturn V rocket, is being transported by plane to NASA's design center.

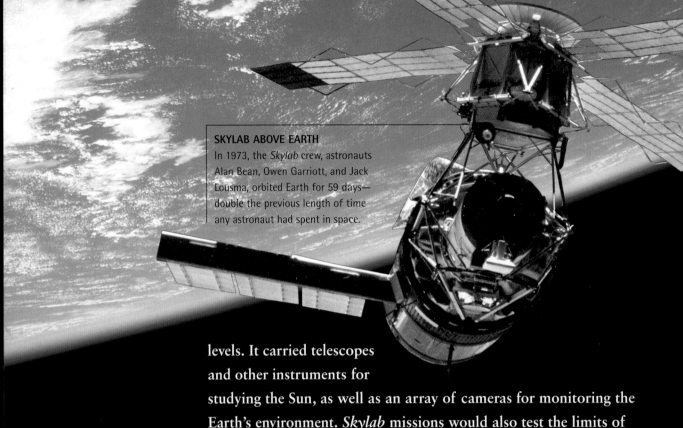

levels. It carried telescopes
and other instruments for
studying the Sun, as well as an array of cameras for monitoring the
Earth's environment. *Skylab* missions would also test the limits of
human endurance in space.

SKYLAB LAUNCH
A Saturn V rocket
launched the uncrewed
Skylab into orbit from the
Kennedy Space Center,
Florida, on May 14, 1973.
The first crew joined
Skylab 11 days later.

Skylab was sent up uncrewed on a Saturn V rocket—the last time
that this class of rocket was ever used—in May 1973. During the
launch, a meteorite shield shook loose and severely damaged one of
the solar panels designed to provide power for the orbiting space
station. Eleven days later, astronauts Charles Conrad, Joseph Kerwin,
and Paul Weitz flew to the crippled station in an Apollo spacecraft to
make repairs and conduct the first experiments. Meanwhile, they
were monitored for the effects of zero gravity. They spent a record
28 days in space, and, on return to the Earth, it was discovered that
the experience had indeed harmed them. Although the astronauts
had used an exercise cycle, weightlessness had still caused problems.
Without the familiar pressure of gravity, little-used muscles had lost
tissue. Bones, too, had changed through lack of use—they shed
calcium in normal conditions, but in space, the calcium loss had
rendered them frail. Changes in hormone levels had resulted in a
loss of red blood cells. It seemed, then, that outer space was
positively dangerous to human life.

The doctors at NASA contemplated the problem, and came up with a program of rigorous physical exercises designed to counteract the effects of free-floating inside *Skylab*. So when the next mission was launched to the craft a month later, the three astronauts were able to remain there for 59 days without any significant ill effects. A third mission was launched in November 1973, and this time its crew lived in *Skylab* for 84 days. It was the longest time ever spent in space, and it included over 22 hours of spacewalking. This was precisely what *Skylab* had been designed for—to determine whether men were ever to be launched toward Mars, or to settle on the Moon. It now seemed that long crewed space flights were indeed a possibility.

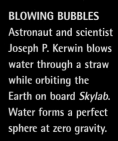

BLOWING BUBBLES
Astronaut and scientist Joseph P. Kerwin blows water through a straw while orbiting the Earth on board *Skylab*. Water forms a perfect sphere at zero gravity.

Skylab had enough provisions for only three crews—there was no way to resupply it—and, in 1979, the empty vessel fell back to Earth, scattering its debris across the Indian Ocean and western Australia. The lessons of the program would be applied to the International Space Station, or ISS, first proposed in the 1980s. This would be a joint venture by Russia and several European nations, as well as the United States. The sheer enormity and cost of the project ensured, however, that it would not take shape until many years later.

EXTRAVEHICULAR ACTIVITY
Astronaut Jack Lousma performs a spacewalk outside the *Skylab* space station. His face is obscured by a beautiful reflection of the Earth.

The progress of the Skylab program was, of course, closely monitored by the Soviets, who were now deeply involved in the Salyut project. *Salyuts 1* and *2* had failed, but in the summer of 1974, shortly after *Skylab*'s final manned mission, the Soviets launched

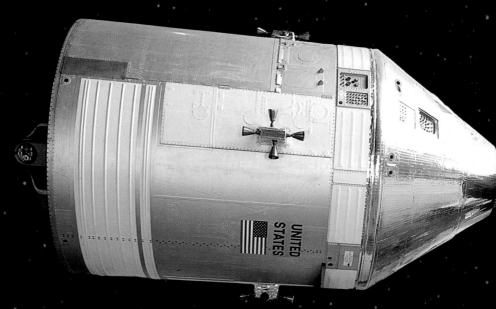

STAR WARS
Science fiction was already imagining space warfare. This almost became a reality when the Soviet Union tested space weapons in the 1970s.

Salyut 3, and two cosmonauts later docked with it. The persistence of Soviet interest in orbiting stations had a political as well as a scientific explanation. The nature of the *Salyut 3* missions has never been fully disclosed, but it seems likely that the cosmonauts were involved in military reconnaissance. One of their main objectives was to locate the positions of American military ships and aircraft, but *Salyut 3* also tracked *Skylab*, proving that it could spy on other spacecraft. *Salyut 3* was equipped with a special gun, the Nudelmann aircraft cannon, that could theoretically be used to attack another spacecraft—space warfare. This sounds too fanciful—too close to the stereotypes of science fiction movies—but the gun was indeed placed on the nose of the craft and tested successfully in space. *Salyut 3* had a planned lifespan of only eight months, and in due course it was deliberately sent into the Earth's atmosphere to burn up.

The presence of weapons in space showed how far relations between the US and the Soviet Union had deteriorated. But the political efforts to reduce this Cold War tension in fact produced a remarkable joint mission. In the summer of 1975, an American Apollo spacecraft docked with a Soviet Soyuz spacecraft, and the two crews mingled. *Soyuz 19* was launched from Baikonur Cosmodrome on July 15, 1975; seven hours later, an Apollo spacecraft left the Kennedy Space Center. In orbit, the American craft gradually closed on the Soyuz, and they

DOCKING STATIONS
The 1975 Apollo-Soyuz Test Project (ASTP) was intended to ease Cold War tensions. A docking module, designed and built by NASA, provided an airlock and transfer corridor between the American Apollo and Soviet Soyuz spacecraft.

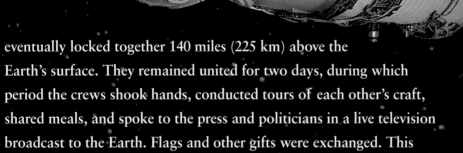

eventually locked together 140 miles (225 km) above the Earth's surface. They remained united for two days, during which period the crews shook hands, conducted tours of each other's craft, shared meals, and spoke to the press and politicians in a live television broadcast to the Earth. Flags and other gifts were exchanged. This marked the first occasion on which the two great space empires cooperated. Although it did not immediately lead to a relaxation of political tensions upon the Earth, it gave hope for a kinder future. Space, after all, was the future.

Through the late 1970s and early 1980s, while the US was concentrating its efforts on developing the space shuttle and on further exploration of

HISTORIC HANDSHAKE
Astronaut Thomas P. Stafford and cosmonaut Aleksey A. Leonov meet halfway between the two docked spacecrafts for an international handshake.

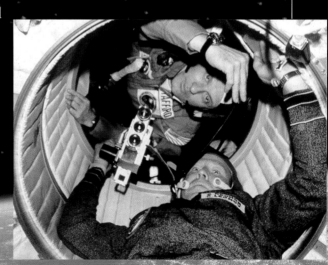

the Solar System, the Soviets' Salyut program
progressed steadily. *Salyut 4*, launched in December 1974,
spent nearly two years in orbit and received two crews. *Salyut 5*,
launched in 1976, was occupied for several months and, in 1977, the
Soviets sent up a new station. *Salyut 6* was host to 16 crews, some of
them non-Soviet, over a period of five years. It was the first station
to have docking facilities at either end, allowing additional crews to
make short visits while another crew was in residence. One dock
could also be used as a port for uncrewed craft carrying fuel, food
and other goods, so that cosmonauts could make extended stays.
Salyut 6 also possessed a restartable rocket engine so that its orbit
could be changed at will. The addition of a module, known as
Cosmos 1267, in 1981 made *Salyut 6* as large as the earlier American
Skylab. This system of modular extension was to become standard
space station practice. *Salyut 6* had facilities for radio and infrared
telescopes, Earth observation cameras, a greenhouse, and furnaces
to make new materials and alloys. It was eventually succeeded by
Salyut 7, which was similar in design to *Salyut 6*. The Salyut project
was altogether a success, and marked a significant step toward the
next Soviet space project, the formidable *Mir* space station. The

Salyut adventure, in fact, emerges as one of the most
enduringly successful of all space enterprises; it did
not have the glamour of the Apollo landings, but it
was remarkable both for its robust technology and
for the human endurance of its crews.

Meanwhile, in deeper space, *Pioneer 11* was voyaging between
Jupiter and Saturn. Having passed Jupiter in 1975, the probe was
accelerated by the force of that planet's gravity on a voyage toward
remote Saturn. Now hurtling at 108,000 miles (173,000 km) per hour,
Pioneer 11 traveled onward for more than four years across a
distance of 1.5 billion miles (2.4 billion km) until, in 1979, it reached
this distant planet with its mysterious rings. *Pioneer 11*'s
readings confirmed that there is indeed more than one ring.
Voyagers 1 and *2* later discovered that there are actually
thousands of rings, but seen from a distance they merge
into a whole. They consist of small particles of rock and ice,
imprisoned within the orbit of the planet. *Voyager 1* also
found that the surface of Titan, the largest of Saturn's moons,
had a substantial atmosphere—the only moon in the Solar
System that does. This so intrigued scientists that, in 1997,
another spacecraft, *Cassini*, was launched to meet the moon.
NASA plans to send down a small probe, named *Huygens*, to the
surface of Titan itself. The hazy clouds on Titan are too thick to
see through, so it is impossible to anticipate what will be
discovered. The actual nature of the moon will be a revelation.
The probe may land in a sea of liquid gas or on solid ice; it has
been constructed for both possibilities. Although Titan is too cold
to support life as we know it, scientists think that its atmosphere
may be similar to that on Earth billions of years ago. If so,
Cassini-Huygens could discover clues to the origins of life itself.

TITAN
Saturn's moon Titan
is larger and heavier
than the planet Pluto.
Voyager 1 discovered that
it had an atmosphere of
nitrogen and methane.

TITAN ADVENTURES
This artist's impression
shows NASA's *Cassini*
spacecraft in orbit
around Saturn's
moon Titan.

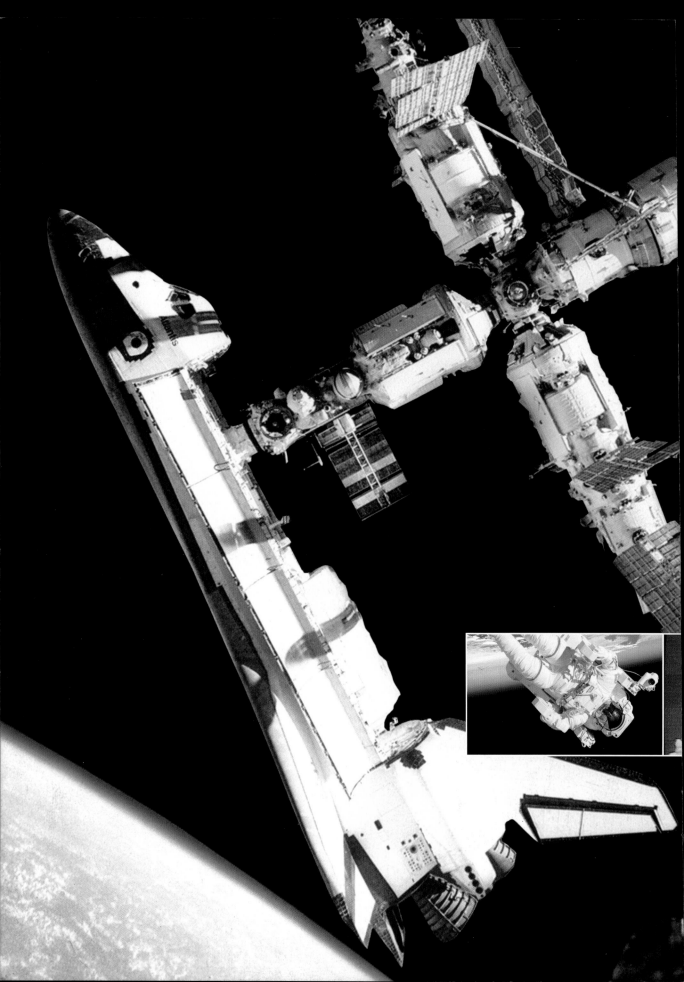

CHAPTER NINE

Living *in* space

With the launch of the US space shuttle and the Soviet space station Mir, astronauts began to spend longer periods of time in space. Living in zero gravity was to prove an entertaining but chaotic experience.

On April 12, 1981, exactly 20 years after Yuri Gagarin's first orbit around the Earth, the space shuttle *Columbia* was launched on its first test flight. The two-day test mission was a success. After further test flights, NASA declared the space shuttle—the world's first reusable space vehicle—operational in July

1982. The notion of a reusable space shuttle had first been put forward by German rocket pioneer Wernher von Braun in the 1940s, but the concept had been far in advance of its time. NASA returned to the idea in 1969, as part of its larger ambition to build a permanent space station. But the first designs for the space shuttle and the space station were both too expensive. So NASA came back with a fresh shuttle design, remarketing the craft as a "space truck" for launching and repairing satellites and for conducting experiments in orbit. In 1972,

its development was finally approved. The new orbiter looked like an aircraft, but it would take off vertically from a launch pad, boosted by two huge solid-fuel rockets. Though the shuttle would go on to become a successful space venture in many ways, its track record was to be marred by twin tragedies: the losses of the *Challenger* and *Columbia* orbiters and their crews. But in the spring of 1981, that first mission seemed to mark the dawn of a spectacular new era of space travel.

The orbiter interior combines work-stations, sleep-stations, food-stations, and leisure-stations. It must be like living and working in a small airliner. Much of the fuselage is given over to the large cargo bay, some 60 x 15 ft (19 x 5 m), in which the instruments or modules to be taken into space or back to the Earth are stored. As well as a pilot and commander, each crew includes up to five specialists—scientists, technicians, or engineers who are experts in handling the mission's cargo or working in a space laboratory.

Most shuttle missions last between five and ten days. Their goals include repairs to orbiting satellites, the launching of solar and planetary probes, the release and repair of space telescopes including the Hubble Space Telescope, and the construction of the International Space Station. One of the most useful scientific payloads has been *Spacelab*, a unit that was installed in the cargo bay. It was used to carry out a wide range of experiments, from the measurement of solar radiation to the exposure of microorganisms in the harsh, alien environment of space. But some of the most valuable studies in space have been those on the human body itself

REUSABLE ORBITER
Space shuttle orbiters, such as *Endeavour*, shown here, are roughly as large as a midsize commercial airliner. Shuttle orbiters have heat-resistant tiles that protect them from the intense heat of reentry into the Earth's atmosphere.

Endeavour

Space shuttle

By the late 1960s, NASA began looking for reusable alternatives to space capsules. The idea was to build a "space plane," and by March 1972, the space shuttle's final design had been approved. The shuttle was made up of three parts: a reusable plane called an orbiter, two solid fuel rockets, also reusable, and a large, throwaway fuel tank. This design means it can be launched as a rocket, and then glide back to Earth like a plane to land on a runway.

After 8 minutes and 58 seconds, the external tank separates from the orbiter and burns up in the atmosphere.

Orbiter stays in space for 5–10 days.

Two minutes and six seconds after liftoff, the solid rocket boosters are discarded. They parachute down to Earth and are recovered to be reused.

Space shuttle blasts off.

Orbiter glides in to land on a 2.8-mile- (4.5-km-) long runway.

Orbiter reenters the Earth's atmosphere. The friction causes intense heat.

NASA has monitored all shuttle crews to see how they adapt to weightlessness, ultimately to prepare humans for future long space voyages.

From 1982 to 2003, there were more than a hundred successful space shuttle missions, during which astronauts extended and increased their skills. Spacewalks, in which a suited-up astronaut maneuvers outside the orbiter in open space, were once considered a dangerous activity. They have now become routine affairs, even though they still need to be carefully choreographed—in a giant swimming pool—months before a mission. Most importantly, the shuttle changed the concept of space travel by making it open to non-astronauts. About 400 people have entered space in the shuttle, including doctors, pilots, engineers, politicians, and scientists.

ROCKET MAN
Astronaut Bruce McCandless spacewalks using a joystick-controlled, jet-propelled backpack.

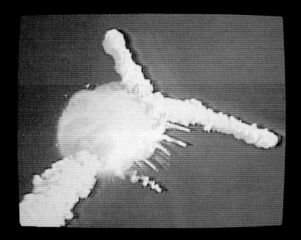

ASPACE SHUTTLE DISASTER
TV viewers watched in horror as *Challenger* exploded
seconds after launch, killing all seven crew members.

A schoolteacher, Christa McAuliffe, was among the seven crew members who entered the space shuttle *Challenger* on January 28, 1986. She had beaten more than 11,000 other applicants in a national competition, run by NASA, to place the first "Teacher in Space." But her triumph would be cut short. Just 73 seconds after *Challenger* left the launch pad at Kennedy Space Center, the shuttle blew apart in a fireball of liquid oxygen and hydrogen. Within 15 seconds it had disintegrated, with the loss of the entire crew. The tragedy unfolded in front of live television audiences.

There was a profound sense of shock. With its solid track record, the space shuttle had come to represent the predictable and reliable space transportation of the future. The disaster was the first in-flight loss of astronauts in the entire history of the US space program. The shuttle program was delayed for two and a half years while NASA examined the reasons for the disaster. They learned that a rubber seal on one of the rocket boosters had been hardened by overnight frost. It had failed on launch, allowing ignition flames to burn into the liquid-propellant tank. But investigators agreed that the real fault lay with mismanagement. Rigorous safety checks, which had been allowed to slide, were brought back. NASA redesigned the rocket booster and commissioned a replacement orbiter, *Endeavour*.

Less than a month after the *Challenger* accident, the grounded Americans could only watch in frustration as the Soviets conducted a launch that was to revolutionize living in space. On February 20, 1986, a 40-ft- (12.4-m-) long module was launched from the Baikonur Cosmodrome. It was the first of seven modules that would, year by year, be pieced together in space like a vast model or aerial sculpture, to become the Soviet Union's eighth space station, called *Mir* (Russian for "peace"). By 1996, the space station had grown to 140 ft (43 m).

The pictures from *Mir* displayed a cozy, if cluttered, environment. Its interior has been compared to a railroad car large enough to accommodate between two and six crew members. This was a Russian home in space. Or, perhaps, a Russian village that had grown haphazardly over the years of its occupation. The cosmonauts mostly wore casual clothing. There were photographs of family and friends, letters, toys, games. There was junk everywhere, the remains of forgotten computers and discarded instruments. There were pools

of grease. There was rust. There were strange smells. *Mir* was dusty—and dust floats in zero gravity, so it has to be vacuumed out of the air. Yet *Mir* was home. One visiting US astronaut remembered that "it seemed there was always music playing, some type of Russian folk music. There were things everywhere, very cluttered—cameras, cables, experiments, personal items." It was by no means the clean and cool environment of the spacecraft pictured in science fiction movies; this was real human life.

There were, of course, many problems. *Mir* remained in orbit for a long time—from 1986 to 2001—so emergencies of one kind or another were inevitable. There were fires, starting suddenly and spectacularly. One serious fire broke out on February 23, 1997, and since there is no up or down in space, it spread evenly and quickly in all directions. The fire was brought under control by extinguishers, but the danger had been acute. There were other problems: humidifiers ceased to work, equipment was bedeviled by short-circuits, and computer programs crashed. Then, just four months after the fire, a robot vehicle collided with one of *Mir*'s modules, *Spektr*. The crew shut down *Spektr* at once and sealed off its hatchway with an emergency pressure cover. If it had not been for their quick action, the crew would have had to abandon *Mir* altogether and take off for Earth in the Soyuz space vehicle, which was always ready in case of such an emergency.

Yet *Mir* survived this and every other hazard and setback. Then, in 1991, the Soviet Union collapsed after 70 years of communist rule, and the Russian Federation came struggling to life. Under the new regime, *Mir* was finally removed from orbit in the spring of 2001. The huge sums of money needed to keep it operational could no longer be justified now that there was no Soviet superpower.

MIR CRYSTAL GROWTH
Space stations allowed astronauts to carry out scientific experiments at zero gravity. Below are a selection of crystals of various proteins that were grown aboard *Mir*.

Mir was the first space vehicle since *Skylab* and the Salyuts to enable astronauts to spend long periods in space. Some cosmonauts stayed in orbit continuously for over a year; others, in a number of missions, totaled more than two years in space. To work in a space station, or on a shuttle, is rather like living in Alice's Wonderland. At any one time, some people may be standing on the ceiling while others are jogging on the walls. Someone may be having a meal beneath you, while someone else passes over your head. On return to Earth, one astronaut tried to put his glass down in midair. Of course, it fell and smashed. In space the glass would have floated beside him, but he had not become used to gravity again. Yet there are reminders of Earth laws: every astronaut must carry a passport in case he or she accidentally lands in foreign territory after reentry to the Earth. Most crew members, on both space stations and the shuttle, experience space-sickness to a greater or lesser degree, so there is a large supply of sick-bags. Weightlessness also has more curious consequences. Without the compressing effect of gravity, an astronaut's spine grows longer, causing considerable backaches. "I noticed in the first four days of my flight," one crew member of the space shuttle recorded, "that muscles in my legs were twitching, firing all the time. My brain wasn't getting any input from my muscles, and it was like it was saying, 'Hey, where's gravity?'"

MIGHTY MIR
Mir space station was built up gradually with seven different modules. Four compartments made up a central core section that contained the living and operational quarters.

SLEEPING IN SPACE
Once used to the strange sensations of zero gravity, sleeping, in any position, can be possible. Here, *Challenger* astronauts get a chance to relax.

HUGE HAIR DAY
While working in space, astronauts still find time to relax and play. Often just exploring the effects of zero gravity can make for amusing crew photographs.

During their first days in space, most astronauts also find it hard to sleep. The physical procedure of sleeping can be difficult in itself; it is necessary to be tethered to a specific site or to be wedged in some convenient corner. Having evolved on Earth, the human body has become accustomed to the restraining effect of gravity, like a prisoner who has become used to his cell.

The food in space is mostly dried and revived with water. One of the curious facts about prolonged space living is that the sense of taste is lost, so that highly spiced food becomes the most desirable. On *Mir*, some astronauts even poured hot sauce on their breakfast cornflakes. Drinks are kept in sealed packages. On the toilet, astronauts are strapped in, and an air-flow system removes body wastes. All these are minor discomforts compared with the one major problem of noise. Living in space is a very noisy affair, with thermal system pumps and air-conditioner compressors, computer hardware fans and various intermittent loud noises from other equipment. The noise is such a problem that some astronauts even suffer temporary hearing damage. Yet when a vehicle has been completely shut down, its systems stopped, the silence has been described as painful. Those astronauts who have worked in these conditions—during temporary power loss, for example—agree that the silence or space is a fearful thing. It is an infinite silence, continuing to the outermost bounds of the Universe, overwhelming that small ball of sound known as the Earth.

Most of a crew's time on a space station or shuttle is devoted to work, experiments, repairs, and the daily filling in of the log. Yet there are always hours reserved for exercise and recreation, for reading or for writing, for playing music, for writing emails on laptop computers. There are games in space, although often they must be played to completely new sets of rules. One game, for example, involves magnetic marbles, which float freely through the air and attract or repel one another upon meeting. Yet the most wonderful recreation of all is simply observation—gazing out of the portholes at the Universe. The astronauts can see shooting stars beneath them. They can observe—almost touch—the darkness and silence of space. But they look, especially, at the ball of blue light that is the Earth. It is an iridescent thing, glowing alone in the Universe. "When I'm looking at living cells in a microscope," wrote Millie Hughes-Fulford, a scientist on board the space shuttle, "they have a glow to them that dead cells don't. And the whole planet has that iridescence of life about it." It is the light of life itself, glistening through a million different forms. The Earth's brightness is rain and wind, forests and oceans. Vast tumultuous fields of light are lightning storms illuminating the canopies of clouds. A great band of smoke and dust is a volcano in eruption. Parts of the Earth flash in a thousand different colors, or are swathed in shimmering green as the southern or northern lights display themselves.

FLOATING FOOD
Mealtimes take some getting used to in space. Astronauts need to be careful not to let their food float away.

WHAT A VIEW
On board the International Space Station, astronaut Ellen Ochoa takes time out to marvel at the view of Earth far below.

CHAPTER TEN

Distant galaxies

The Voyager probes continued their incredible journeys, enriching our knowledge of the planets. With the aid of orbiting telescopes, we could now look into deep space, too.

A lthough the manned space missions provided plenty of excitement and drama for the public, of equal interest to the scientists were the unmanned probes sent to investigate the planets of the Solar System. Through the early 1980s—behind the spectacles of the space shuttle's debut, the *Challenger* tragedy, and the development of *Mir*—the two interplanetary Voyager probes had been silently moving away from Saturn, having previously visited Jupiter and its moons. *Voyager 1* was now departing from Saturn's sphere of influence and advancing into interstellar space. In January 1986, nine years after its launch, *Voyager 2* reached Uranus—the first and, so far, last spacecraft to do so. The probe turned its cameras and antennae on a planet with a canopy of thin haze above an atmosphere stained a delicate blue-green by methane gas. *Voyager 2* detected streaks of

A COMET'S COMA
Jets of gas and dust
spurt out of Halley's
nucleus, or center,
forming a white
cloud called a
coma.

brightness in the cloud cover, a visible
token of methane ice clouds low in the
atmosphere. It produced an excellent image
of the 11 rings that circle the planet, and
discovered 10 new moons. *Voydger 2* then
journeyed on toward Neptune.

Meanwhile, in March 1986, a European probe named
Giotto began a unique journey of discovery toward
Halley's comet. Every 76 years, this ball of rock, ice,
gas, and dust reappears on its endless orbit around the
Sun. Halley's comet comes from the Kuiper Belt, a ring of
icy objects (called Kuiper Belt objects) each a few
hundred miles across. On occasions, a Kuiper
object moves toward the Sun and is heated to the
point at which it expels a trail of gas and dust
known as a coma; it becomes a comet. There
are perhaps 70,000 Kuiper objects, of which
only 650 have ever been identified.
Future space probes will help to
account for their mysteries.

Giotto's journey was described
as a suicide mission, because it was
expected to be destroyed by a high-speed
collision with the fierce storm of dust that
is continually ejected from the core, or
nucleus, of Halley's comet. Giotto went
into the coma around the comet, and its
camera returned images of the comet
until contact was lost after collision
with a particle. These photographs, plus

UNORTHODOX STAR
In Italian artist Giotto di
Bondone's 1305 painting
*The Adoration of the
Magi*, it is thought that
Halley's comet (visible at
top center) was used as a
model for the star of
Bethlehem. The comet
had passed around the
Earth in 1301.

GIOTTO
In 1986, the space
probe *Giotto* was
launched to Halley's
comet. On approach, its
electronic camera took
images every four seconds.

information gathered from other instruments on board, showed that every second, Halley's comet discharges up to 30 tons of dust and vaporized water. Its nucleus is a little world made of ice and rock, some 9 miles (14.5 km) long, and about 5 miles (8 km) wide. It has its own chain of ice hills. The comet hurtles through space in a continual state of eruption and disintegration, discharging gas and dust in its wake. It is a little knot of effervescence that, in the light of the Sun, leaves a pale blue trail. Giotto survived its passage through the coma, although some of its instruments were damaged beyond repair. It traveled onward for another six years before encountering Grigg-Skjellerup, another comet. In 1992, Giotto was shut down and is now in perpetual orbit around the Sun.

The journey of *Voyager 2* was continuing also. It had been traveling for 12 years, covering 4.5 billion miles (7.2 billion km) of space and passing three planets. In 1989, *Voyager 2* reached Neptune, the most distant of our gassy planets and the probe's final rendezvous before it headed for interstellar space. The images *Voyager 2* sent back to Earth show Neptune's deep blue clouds in a state of continual turmoil. The planet is full of storm and whirlwind, more so than any other in the Solar System. The probe detected a huge oval cloud. It was a storm the size of the Earth. Other clouds are streaks of frozen methane. There are hurricanes racing across the planet's surface. Neptune is in perpetual blue movement. *Voyager 2* discovered six new moons of Neptune. It also found that one of those already observed, Triton,

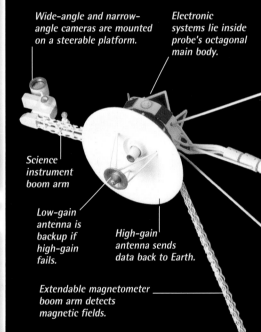

Voyager 2

Built to explore the Solar System's outer planets where sunlight is weak, the *Voyager 2* probe was powered by a radioactive source rather than solar panels. It also needed a larger antenna dish than other probes—12 ft (3.7 m) in diameter—to send back data to Earth from greater distances. Its aim was to fly by Jupiter, Saturn, Uranus, and Neptune, and investigate their characteristics, atmospheres, moons, and rings, as well as determining magnetic fields.

Wide-angle and narrow-angle cameras are mounted on a steerable platform.

Electronic systems lie inside probe's octagonal main body.

Science instrument boom arm

Low-gain antenna is backup if high-gain fails.

High-gain antenna sends data back to Earth.

Extendable magnetometer boom arm detects magnetic fields.

DECEPTIVE LOOKS
Despite its tranquil appearance, Neptune is characterized by ferocious storms and freezing winds. Its blue color comes from a small amount of the gas methane in the atmosphere.

had some peculiar characteristics. The surface temperature is −391 °F (−235 °C), making Triton the coldest known object in the entire Solar System. It is a truly alien landscape of frozen nitrogen methane. Yet it is not still. Vast eruptions of gas send up immense clouds of dust and ice particles.

While probes such as the *Voyagers* contribute to our knowledge of the planets, orbiting observatories closer to home provide extraordinary insights into deep space. These include the highly successful Hubble Space Telescope. Unlike ground telescopes, whose view of space is clouded and distorted by the Earth's atmosphere, the Hubble gives scientists a uniquely clear view of the Universe. It was launched on the space shuttle in the spring of 1990 and placed in orbit about 372 miles (600 km) above the Earth, where it has been operating ever since. Most satellites are built to last only a few years. But the Hubble, intended to last until 2010, was designed for maintenance and repair by shuttle crews. Astronauts can replace worn-out equipment, fit more advanced instruments, and nudge the satellite back into higher orbit whenever it sinks toward the Earth. On the first service mission, in 1993, a shuttle crew repaired the main telescope mirror, which had been wrongly manufactured and gave an out-of-focus image. The Hubble is controlled by computer on Earth, and is used by hundreds of

STAR BIRTH
These huge gas and dust pillars, or nebulas, are star nurseries. Inside the tiny fingers at their tops, hydrogen is contracting and turning into new stars.

astronomers in many different countries, their work coordinated by the Space Telescope Science Institute in the United States.

The Hubble Space Telescope has photographed the birth of stars and the merging of galaxies. It has taken pictures of globular clusters of stars, of double stars, of open clusters of stars, and of the exploded stars known as supernovas. It has sent back images of a supernova that looks like a giant eye in space. It has found evidence of the existence of other solar systems and of black holes—collapsed stars with such powerful gravity that anything that comes near them, including light, is swallowed up. The star nearest to our Solar System is Proxima Centauri, 4.2 light-years away. The nearest nebula, Orion, is 1,500 light-years away.

OBSERVING SPACE
The Hubble Space Telescope was launched in 1990 to observe the infrared, optical, and ultraviolet Universe. It was named after US astronomer Edwin Hubble who, in 1929, was the first to establish that the Universe is expanding.

The Hubble Space Telescope

Launched in 1990, the Hubble Space Telescope captures stunning images of galaxies, nebulas, and clusters, without distortions from the Earth's atmosphere. Its main mirror has a diameter of 8 ft (2.4 m) and the whole telescope is 43 ft (13.1 m) long. Regularly serviced and modified by spacewalking astronauts, Hubble is controlled remotely from NASA's Goddard Space Flight Center in Maryland. It is known as a reflecting telescope—light enters it, bounces off a mirror, and reflects back to a detector. A radio antenna then relays the data back to Earth via a satellite system.

Solar panels turn sunlight into electricity to power the telescope.

Instruments detect and measure incoming light.

Primary concave mirror captures incoming rays of light and directs them toward the secondary mirror.

Incoming light rays

Secondary convex mirror reflects the rays onto the instruments.

WHIRLPOOL GALAXY

A Hubble image of a whirlpool galaxy known as M51, about 20 million light-years away from the Earth. The red areas are starbirth regions, and the yellow center contains older stars.

But Hubble looks far beyond even them, into the regions of unimaginable time and space. It has recorded images of galaxies some 10 billion light-years away. The Milky Way galaxy, our Solar System's home in the Universe, holds some 200 billion stars, but this is only one galaxy among about 40 that make up what is known as the local group. This local group of galaxies is, in turn, one of several galaxy clusters that make up the local supercluster. And there are millions of these superclusters, stretching out through billions of light-years of space. Immensity is piled upon immensity. The mind and the imagination break down before the enormity. The light that reaches us from these celestial bodies has been traveling from its

source for billions of years; to record this ancient light is to look back into the immeasurable caverns of time.

HOME IN THE UNIVERSE

The Milky Way galaxy is thought to be more than 100,000 light-years wide. Our Solar System is 25,000 light-years from the galactic center. Although the Milky Way is a spiral-shaped galaxy, seen from the inside, as here, it looks like a mass of densely packed stars.

Until the age of space exploration, we could only observe the Universe from the ground using visible light. Modern space observatories, however, can see what the human eye cannot; they identify, and make images from, many other wavelengths of radiation, such as gamma-ray, ultraviolet, X-ray, and most of the infrared range. These wavelengths cannot be detected from the Earth, because they are absorbed by our atmosphere. So to have an observatory in space clarifies everything. One such example is the Compton Gamma Ray Observatory, which was designed to detect and observe gamma rays, giving scientists

SUPERNOVA
When giant stars die, they explode, becoming supernovas. These are so bright that they can outshine entire galaxies.

new insights into their mysterious sources. Gamma rays are a form of high-energy radiation produced by the violent events of the Universe, such as supernovas—the remnants of exploded, dying stars. A series of space observatories has been designed to detect relatively cool objects, which emit invisible infrared radiation.

As the Universe expands, galaxies older than our own move away from us at increasing speed. As they accelerate, the visible light they emit is stretched to longer, reddish wavelengths—just as the sound waves from a police siren change in pitch as it passes you

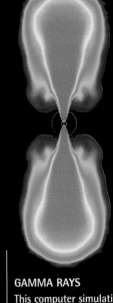

GAMMA RAYS
This computer simulation shows jets of particles (red) spewing from the core of a supernova. The jets are sources of gamma rays.

SPACE LAUNCH
This photograph shows the Gamma Ray Observatory being launched by the Remote Manipulator System from the shuttle *Atlantis* in April 1991. The observatory operated until 2000.

and moves away at high speed. The most distant galaxies are traveling away from us so quickly that almost all of their light has been shifted beyond the red extreme of the visible region (so that our eyes cannot see it) and into the infrared.

By looking at distant objects in infrared, scientists can learn more about the origins of the Universe. Infrared sensors have been added to the Hubble, but its successor, the James Webb Telescope, will observe only in the infrared. The Webb will look for the oldest and most distant galaxies—the first to emerge out of the darkness, just a few hundred million years after the Universe began. Another observatory, the Cosmic Background Explorer, launched in 1989, measured both microwave and infrared radiation. It detected what may be the remaining energy from the Big Bang explosion itself. This shows up as a faint background hum of radiation throughout space. It is a trace of the origin of the Universe, an echo of the beginning.

X-ray telescopes detect rays created by objects with a temperature of more than a million degrees. X-rays are thrown out by supernovas (exploding stars), and from quasars—ancient, distant galaxies where matter is heated to millions of degrees as it spirals into a central black hole. Today's X-ray telescopes include the immensely powerful

CORONAL LOOPS
This image shows coronal loops of hot gas on the Sun's surface. The heating of the Sun's atmosphere is due to the tangling of magnetic fields—the hot gas follows the magnetic field lines.

XMM-Newton, which detects very hot objects created early in the life of the Universe.

To help scientists understand how the Sun makes energy, the space observatories Ulysses, SOHO, and TRACE stare continuously at our star. They trace different orbits, and Ulysses has a unique vantage point when it passes over the Sun's poles. Deep inside the Sun, hydrogen is converted into helium by nuclear reactions. These release vast amounts of energy. Each photon, or particle, of energy takes 30,000 years to reach the surface, and eight minutes to reach the Earth as light and heat. It has been calculated that one second of the Sun's energy, if it could be harnessed, would power the world for a thousand years. The observatories measure the many kinds of radiation that come from our star. They look at ripples in the Sun's surface, or photosphere. They study the Sun's atmosphere and the constant stream of particles emitted, known as the solar wind. They locate the causes of solar flares—terrific, concentrated outbursts of energy from the Sun's atmosphere. They also describe how the Sun interacts with the Earth. Stormy solar weather can, for example, damage satellites and harm astronauts; it may even affect high-flying aircraft. The observatories are our early-warning systems.

"Mankind has a thirst for knowledge. Why are we going to do this?" observed one scientist, working on one of the observatories. "Because we haven't done it before and we want to understand more. That's just the curiosity of mankind." It is also the central principle behind space observation and exploration—the human need to reach out toward the stars, and to understand the Universe in which we have, perhaps fortuitously, emerged.

THE SUN
This ultraviolet image of the Sun was taken by the SOHO satellite. Around the Sun's edge are eruptions of superhot gases escaping the star's gravity.

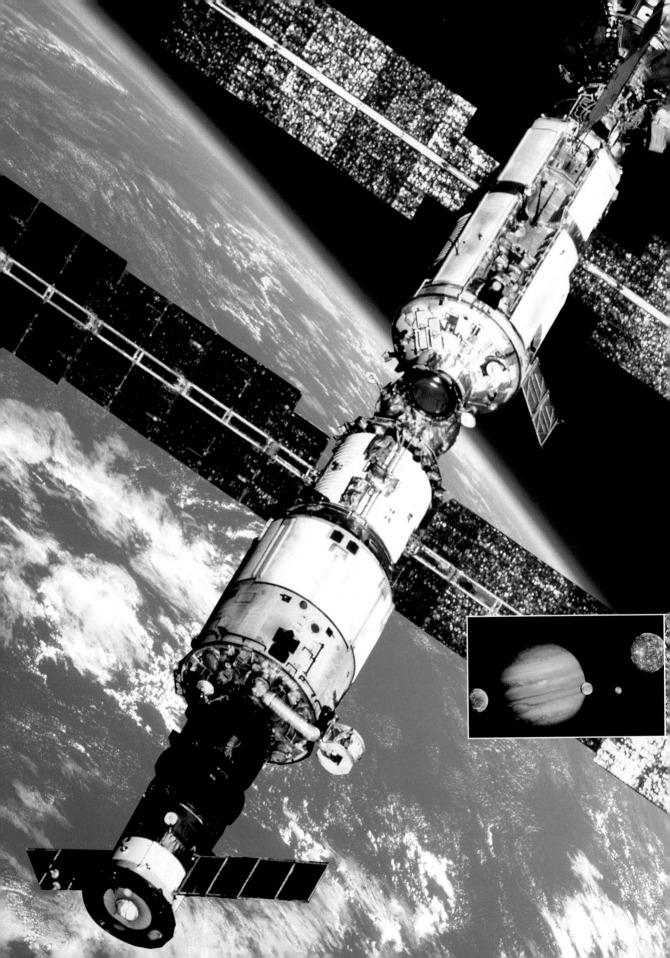

CHAPTER ELEVEN

Colonizing space

*In the 1990s, the ancient dream of creating
a city in the sky began, at last, to be realized,
as construction started on the long-awaited
International Space Station. Meanwhile, the
quest to find life in our Solar System continued.*

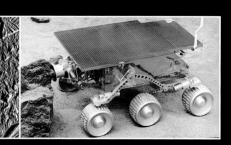

The human yearning for knowledge, and the appetite for distant exploration, bore new fruit at the end of the 20th century. In 1993, the United States and Russia signed a joint space treaty. US vice-president Al Gore declared that "after years of competition in space, which symbolized the rivalry between our nations, we have found a common destiny in cooperation and partnership, a cooperation in space which symbolizes the cooperation we are building here on Earth." Once more, politics extended its influence into space exploration. The two countries would work together in the fields of "space science, space exploration, space applications, and the use of space technology." The treaty also paved the way for the construction of the International Space Station (ISS). There had been plans for such a project since 1984, but no hardware had been forthcoming.

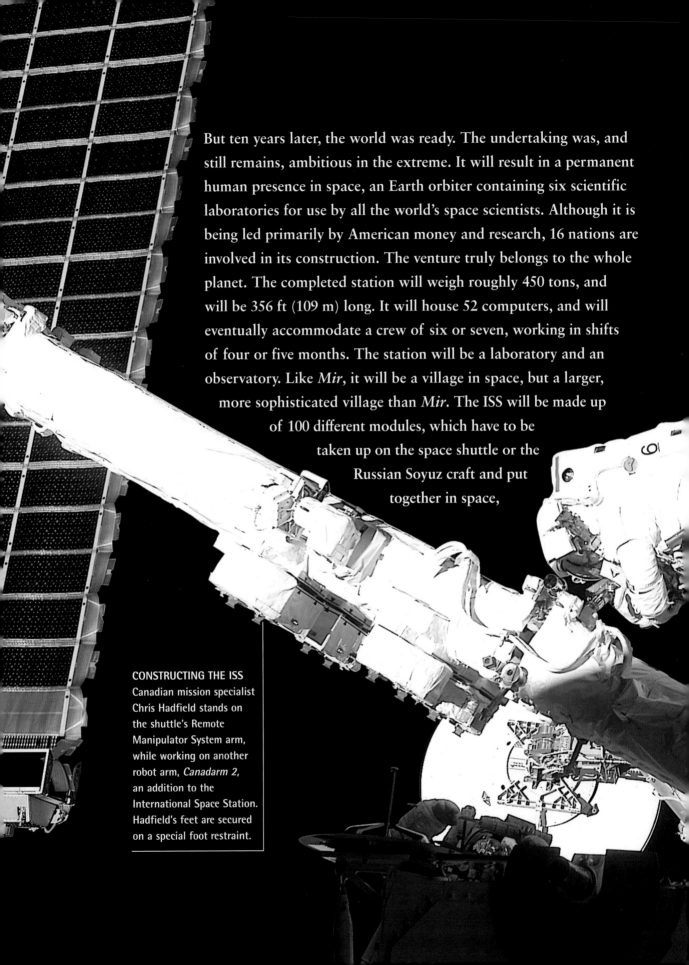

But ten years later, the world was ready. The undertaking was, and still remains, ambitious in the extreme. It will result in a permanent human presence in space, an Earth orbiter containing six scientific laboratories for use by all the world's space scientists. Although it is being led primarily by American money and research, 16 nations are involved in its construction. The venture truly belongs to the whole planet. The completed station will weigh roughly 450 tons, and will be 356 ft (109 m) long. It will house 52 computers, and will eventually accommodate a crew of six or seven, working in shifts of four or five months. The station will be a laboratory and an observatory. Like *Mir*, it will be a village in space, but a larger, more sophisticated village than *Mir*. The ISS will be made up of 100 different modules, which have to be taken up on the space shuttle or the Russian Soyuz craft and put together in space,

CONSTRUCTING THE ISS
Canadian mission specialist Chris Hadfield stands on the shuttle's Remote Manipulator System arm, while working on another robot arm, *Canadarm 2,* an addition to the International Space Station. Hadfield's feet are secured on a special foot restraint.

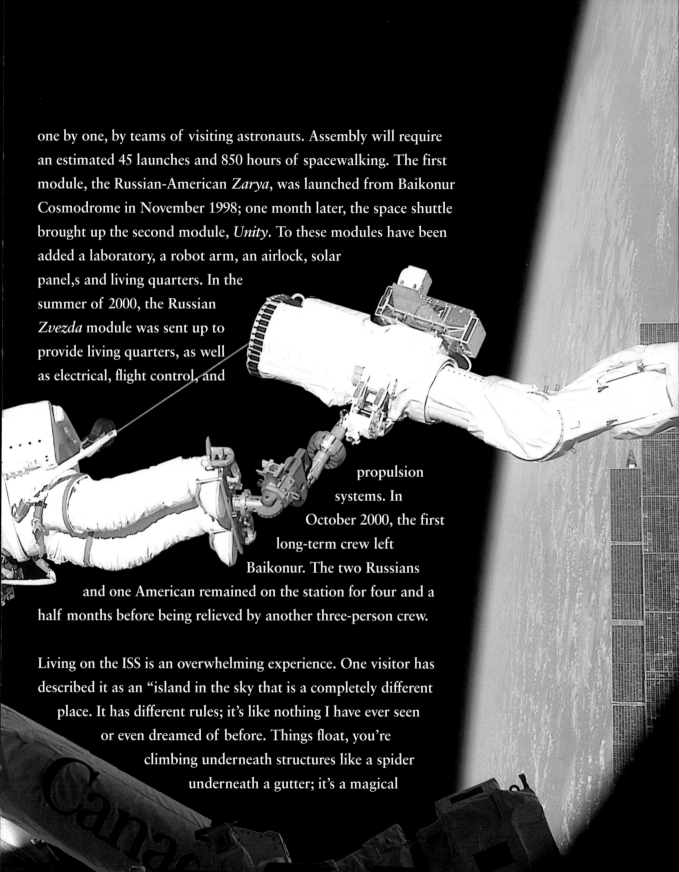

one by one, by teams of visiting astronauts. Assembly will require
an estimated 45 launches and 850 hours of spacewalking. The first
module, the Russian-American *Zarya*, was launched from Baikonur
Cosmodrome in November 1998; one month later, the space shuttle
brought up the second module, *Unity*. To these modules have been
added a laboratory, a robot arm, an airlock, solar
panel,s and living quarters. In the
summer of 2000, the Russian
Zvezda module was sent up to
provide living quarters, as well
as electrical, flight control, and

propulsion
systems. In
October 2000, the first
long-term crew left
Baikonur. The two Russians
and one American remained on the station for four and a
half months before being relieved by another three-person crew.

Living on the ISS is an overwhelming experience. One visitor has
described it as an "island in the sky that is a completely different
place. It has different rules; it's like nothing I have ever seen
or even dreamed of before. Things float, you're
climbing underneath structures like a spider
underneath a gutter; it's a magical

place." It is estimated that this magical island in the sky will probably be completed by 2007. It has already become a familiar sight in the night skies, a lasting token of human presence in space.

Back in 1989, long before the ISS had begun to take form, the spacecraft *Galileo* had been launched from the space shuttle on an extraordinary voyage that would terminate on Jupiter. The craft had been named in recognition of the Italian 17th-century scientist Galileo Galilei, who was the first to observe Jupiter's four largest moons—Io, Ganymede, Callisto and Europa. Once more we honor the past in our quest toward the future. *Galileo* could not reach Jupiter by rocket power alone, but needed help from other sources—the planets themselves. The probe flew past Venus, returned to Earth, headed out into the asteroid belt, and returned again to Earth before finally heading for Jupiter. Each planetary encounter provided an increase in velocity, enabling *Galileo* to travel faster. During the early phase of its journey, *Galileo* passed near two asteroids—Gaspra in 1991, and Ida in 1993. Ida was found to have a tiny moon orbiting it. In 1995, *Galileo* eventually reached Jupiter and delivered a probe, which hurtled into the upper

HOT TARGET

The *Galileo* space probe started its 6-year journey to Jupiter in October 1989. In December 1995, it finally arrived at the planet. When *Galileo* entered Jupiter's atmosphere, it had to endure a temperature more than twice that of the Sun.

JUPITER'S MOONS

Jupiter's massive gravity holds 61 moons, although most of these are small, asteroid-like boulders. The smallest is just a few miles across. The four largest moons are Ganymede, Callisto, Io, and Europa, sometimes called the Galilean moons. They can all be seen from the Earth with just binoculars.

Jupiter

Ganymede

Europa

atmosphere before opening a parachute to slow its descent. For the next hour, the probe analyzed chemicals in the clouds, transmitting the data back to the orbiting *Galileo*. A huge belt of radiation, thousands of miles above the planet, was studied, and winds of up to 330 miles (530 km) per hour were recorded. As the probe sank deeper, it melted in Jupiter's hot atmosphere. *Galileo* itself will finally melt into the atmosphere also, by which time it will have studied Jupiter and its main moons for almost eight years.

Jupiter's gravity holds 61 moons, many of which have been discovered in recent years by ground-based telescopes. The four main moons came under *Galileo*'s scrutiny between 1995 and 2002. Io is in a state of continual volcanic eruption; it harbors lakes of molten sulfur and layers of molten lava. Ganymede is the largest moon in the Solar System—larger even than the planet Mercury. It has a heavily layered surface of rock and ice and a core of molten iron. Callisto, like our own Moon, is covered with craters. Europa is a sphere of ice enclosing a rocky core. These striking contrasts of fire and ice bring us closer to an understanding of the beginnings of the Solar System itself.

Callisto

Io

Ganymede, Callisto and Europa are all thought to contain saltwater seas beneath their frozen surfaces. An ocean on Europa is of special interest to

SURFACE OF EUROPA
Europa's icy surface has been broken up into plates up to 8.5 miles (13 km) across. The plates have collided with each other, resembling the pack ice that floats on Earth's polar seas. These features suggest that at some point there was water or soft ice beneath the surface.

Understanding asteroids

Between the nine planets of our Solar System lie smashed chunks of rock known as asteroids. Jupiter's mighty gravity forces most of these rocks into a swirling "belt" between Jupiter and Mars. Never managing to fuse together and form planets, asteroids are astronomically tiny—the largest is Ceres, which measures just 580 miles (930 km) across.

Ida uncovered
On its way to Jupiter, the *Galileo* probe photographed Ida. The asteroid's surface shows craters from collisions with smaller rocks.

scientists because it is anticipated to be close enough to the surface to be a potential habitat for life forms. There is a further cause for excitement here: Europa's icy surface is punctuated with cracks and vents, so it is possible that heat and gas from within the moon have penetrated the water, or a meteorite might have plunged into its depths, bringing with it organic (carbon-containing) molecules— the building blocks of life.

The possible existence of an ocean that could contain life beneath Europa's surface was one of the most exciting finds of *Galileo*'s seven years. NASA is hoping to send an orbiter to Europa to find further evidence of this ocean. If it succeeds, an advanced spacecraft may then be sent to peer into the ocean to search for life. To achieve this spectacular feat, it will use a probe with a heated tip to bore through the ice before releasing a robotic submarine into the depths.

The search for life is endless. It lies at the heart of all exploration of space, as if humankind were driven to discover the source and reason for its own existence in the Universe. To this end, the search for life on Mars was revived. In 1996, scientists analyzed a Martian meteorite that had landed some 13,000 years ago in Antarctica. They reported seeing tube-shaped microscopic objects, possibly the fossilized remains of bacteria. The report surprised the scientific community, and its findings are still vigorously debated today. Though no one suggests that it offers proof of the existence of life on Mars, it opens up a tantalizing possibility.

LIFE WITHOUT LIGHT

We now know that life is possible without oxygen or sunlight. In recent years, colonies of bacteria, worms, mollusks, crustaceans and fish have been discovered around deep sea vents, or "black smokers," deep in the Earth's oceans. It is likely that conditions are similar in the oceans of Jupiter's moon Europa and, if so, primitive life forms could exist there, too.

On July 4, 1997, an American spacecraft, *Mars Pathfinder*, landed on the Martian surface. It touched down in a landscape where, it was believed, there had once been a mighty flood. Strewn boulders and rocks implied the impact of some rushing torrent, and rounded stones suggested running water to shape them. *Pathfinder* carried a remotely operated rover, *Sojourner,* which traveled over the dusty, rock-strewn terrain. Each day, *Sojourner* was directed by controllers to a new site where it carried out scientific studies. Both the lander and the rover functioned far longer than predicted, and 2.6 gigabits of electronic data on Martian dust, rock, and the cold Martian wind were transmitted back to Earth.

Since 1997, a satellite called *Global Surveyor* has been orbiting the planet, taking the most detailed pictures yet of the valleys, craters, ice caps, sand dunes, and local weather. In 2001, another satellite, *Mars Odyssey*, began making a meticulous survey of the surface. So far, *Mars Odyssey* has found strong evidence for large amounts of subsurface water. The British-built *Beagle 2* craft is hurtling toward the Red Planet. *Beagle 2* is designed to descend to the surface and search for signs of primitive life. Soon after its arrival, two NASA *Mars Exploration Rovers* will land and explore the terrain at sites suspected to have once supported water, and both NASA and Russia have even produced outline plans for crewed missions to the planet. Very soon, all eyes will be on Mars.

GLOBAL SURVEYOR
Global Surveyor began orbiting Mars in 1997. It carried cameras and spectrometers designed to map the planet in detail and study its weather patterns and chemical composition.

MARS BUGGY
The *Sojourner* rover was delivered onto the surface of Mars by the *Pathfinder* probe on July 4, 1997. Just 24.5 in (63 cm) long, it had six wheels that moved separately, enabling it to negotiate rocks without falling over. Scientists on Earth used the camera on *Pathfinder* to monitor *Sojourner*, but the rover could use its own cameras to find its way around.

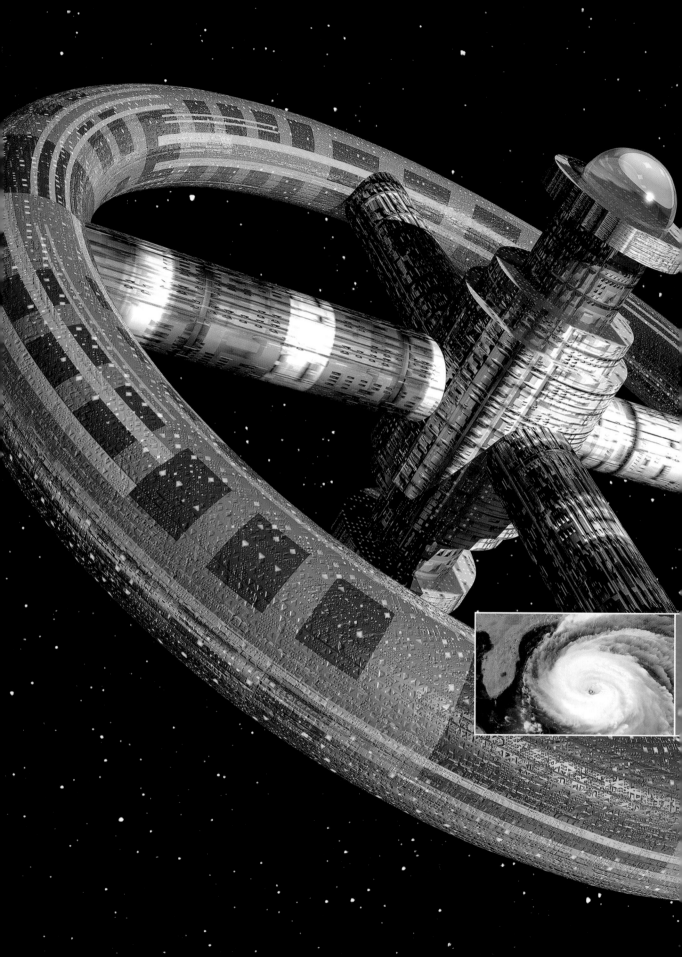

CHAPTER TWELVE

The future in space

In the 21st century, the relentless drive to explore space continues unabated. More and more sophisticated probes, landers, and observatories are planned to investigate the nearest planets and the farthest galaxies.

The launch of the world's first satellite, *Sputnik 1*, in 1957, was the start of a revolution that, today, we have come to accept as an integral part of human life. There are now hundreds of different kinds of satellites in space, programmed for thousands of different tasks. There are communications satellites, designed to connect all places on the Earth with one another, making the planet like one great echo chamber; there are weather satellites, ready to detect changes in pressure or humidity, to decipher whirlwinds and to predict tempests; there are navigation satellites that can steer ships and even direct cars; there are Earth-resource satellites to observe the polar ice caps or scrutinize the desert wastes; there are military satellites to guide missiles and bombs, or to photograph foreign territory so minutely that a child's shoe can be clearly seen. Some

HURRICANE MONITOR
This image was taken by a NOAA (National Oceanic and Atmospheric Administration) satellite on September 4, 1996. It shows hurricane Fran approaching the North American mainland from the Caribbean Sea.

satellites follow the migrations of birds, blue whales and elephant seals; others measure the amount of volcanic ash or pollution in the atmosphere. Satellites can be used to stalk deer or to trace distress calls from ships and planes. Thanks to the global positioning system, anyone can have their latitude and longitude beamed down from a satellite to a hand-held receiver, enabling them to find their exact position on a map. There are satellites designed to monitor other satellites and to coordinate their activities.

In the near future, they are also to become smaller, faster and cheaper. For example, NASA's Nanosat Constellation Trailblazer (NCT) mission will involve the launch of a "constellation" of three miniature satellites, or "nanosats," each a little larger than a birthday cake. They will work

MAPPING THE WORLD
An Inupiat man checks his location with a global positioning satellite system (GPS) monitor in Alaska. Thanks to the GPS system, the world's wildernesses are a little easier to navigate.

together to observe the effects of the Sun on the Earth. The NCT mission may pave the way for a more ambitious mission to launch a swarm of 100 nanosats circling the Earth.

But there are problems to be considered, chief of which is the huge amount of unwanted matter cluttering space. In December 2002, it was calculated that there were 8,844 articles in Earth's orbit. As well as active satellites, these include outdated satellites, old spacecraft, pieces of exploded rockets, and tools lost by spacewalkers. There are also many thousands of particles of aluminum oxide, the residue of spent rocket fuel. Because they all travel several times faster than a bullet, even the smallest object can have a great effect. The space shuttle is regularly damaged by flecks of paint and other tiny particles. Those objects in high orbit will remain there for millions of years, creating a gigantic junkyard in space. Meanwhile, a division of North American Aerospace Defense Command permanently monitors the debris in space and calculates the probability of any piece colliding with working spacecraft.

SPACE JUNK
This artwork shows the distribution of debris—remnants of the many space missions carried out since the 1950s—in orbit around the Earth. These objects present a potential hazard to future space missions.

IMPACT CRATER STUDY
Scientists study enlarged images of impact craters caused by space debris on a solar panel of the Hubble Space Telescope. Data from such studies is used in the planning of future missions, particularly that of the ISS.

COLUMBIA DISASTER
On February 1, 2003, the space shuttle *Columbia* broke up on reentry into the Earth's atmosphere, instantly killing the crew of seven. Debris from the explosion was scattered over a wide area of the southern US.

THE SHUTTLE FLEET
Columbia, seen here orbiting the Earth, made the first-ever shuttle flight on April 12, 1981. Over the next ten years, it was joined by three sister ships, *Challenger* (1982–6), *Discovery* (1983), and *Atlantis* (1985).

Damage caused by space debris was one of the theories put forward by scientists to explain the second space shuttle disaster. On February 1, 2003, *Columbia* disintegrated on reentry into the Earth's atmosphere, killing all seven of the crew. It appeared that some heat-resistant tiles had come away from the left wing after being struck by debris, either during the launch or while in orbit. If so, the open wound would have allowed super-heated air to rush in and melt the aluminum subframe, sending *Columbia* out of control. The crew of the fatally damaged craft was traveling far too fast and at too high an altitude to parachute to safety by means of the cockpit escape system. This disaster has cast grave doubts over the prospects of long-distance space travel, and possibly the future of the space shuttle itself.

While NASA ponders the future of crewed flight, robotic probes continue their journeys. The *Pioneer* and *Voyager* probes are now heading out of our Solar System into deep space. Each of the four probes carries a message, in case they are found by intelligent alien beings. Though signals from the *Pioneers* can no longer be detected,

the probes carry engraved metal plates displaying the forms of male and female human beings and showing their place within the Solar System. The *Voyager* probes carry gold-plated records (complete with stylus, cartridge, and picture instructions etched on their aluminum covers), which contain the sound of music and of human voices, of the wind and the song of the whales. These echoes of the Earth are drifting into the irrecoverable bounds of space. They will continue on their journeys for millions, perhaps billions, of years. They can still, now, be tracked by NASA's Deep Space Network, but there will come a time when they will be lost to infinity. Then they will become the oldest surviving artifacts ever produced by human beings, monuments of a civilization that, by then, may itself have already faded away.

As these probes disappear into infinity, other missions are already underway, carrying the latest and most sophisticated technology. NASA's New Millennium program is dispatching probes to test technology that can adapt to new situations in flight. The probe *Deep Space 1*, for example, could use its "intelligence" to navigate by studying the positions of the stars. A further probe, *Stardust*, launched in 1999, will use aerogel—an extraordinarily light but strong, spongelike substance—to gather samples of dust from a comet's coma.

In the immediate future, a new wave of uncrewed craft will fly out to the planets and satellites of the Solar System, many of them designed to soft-land and observe at close hand. Three spacecraft, one European and two American, will soon land on Mars.

VOYAGING ON

Launched in 1977, the two *Voyager* probes left the Solar System in 1997. They will reach nearby stars in about 40,000 years. NASA hopes that they will be found by alien civilizations.

INTERSTELLAR RECORD

The *Voyager* probes carry old-fashioned records with recordings of sounds from Earth, including greetings in 56 languages. More than 100 photographs, including this one showing the two human sexes and an unborn child in its mother's womb, are also encoded on the record.

The *Messenger* probe will orbit Mercury—the first spacecraft to do so in more than 25 years. A project called Starlight will test new methods of remote observation. NASA will use the technology tested by *Starlight* when sending its *Terrestrial Planet Finder* into the depths of space. This probe is to seek out other planets moving within other solar systems, and one of its tasks will be to assess their potential for harboring life. These missions form a part of NASA's Origins program, a drive to understand the origins of life and of the Universe itself. The space enterprise is gathering speed and momentum.

And what of that distant future? Crewed flights are still highly dangerous. The risks have been emphasized, unfortunately, by the *Columbia* shuttle disaster. There are plans eventually to land humans on the surface of Mars. But this is a most hazardous undertaking— because of planetary alignments, the astronauts would have to endure one and a half years on the surface before returning home; the surface itself has an atmosphere almost wholly composed of carbon dioxide, and has an average temperature of −63°F (−53°C). It will take many years—many decades—of patient research and technological enterprise to overcome these difficulties. There are also plans to place a hotel in space, so that tourists may orbit the Earth and watch the planet from bars and lounges. Some people hope to build space colonies on the Moon and Mars, with vegetation providing oxygen and food. These colonists of the distant future might be miners, refining the lunar rock for iron or building materials. Or they might be engineers. Large areas of the lunar surface could be coated in cells that gather solar energy, which could then be

INFINITE UNIVERSE
The Milky Way galaxy contains about 200 billion stars, but is just one of billions of galaxies in the Universe. Many scientists believe that it is unlikely we are alone in such immensity, but that it is also unlikely that we will ever be able to travel far enough to find out. The farther galaxies are moving away from us so fast that we would need a time machine to reach them.

beamed back to the Earth in order to supply our growing need for energy. Humans might mine asteroids for their minerals at some future date. There are even proposals for the crewed exploration of more distant space, beyond our Solar System, using engines powered by lasers or even by antimatter. There is even talk of a warp-drive that would expand and contract space, but this is still at the stage of speculation; science has yet to catch up with fantasy.

And then, of course, there is also the possibility of some future discovery of life on other planets in the farther reaches of space. Such a possibility would change the nature of human life on the Earth. This is the beginning, not the end. The adventure continues.

Space Exploration

THE LAUNCH OF SPUTNIK 1, the first human-made object to orbit the Earth, marked the start of the space age in 1957. Since then, humankind has achieved many extraordinary feats in space, including landing humans on the Moon. Here are some of the major landmarks.

Satellites and Observatories

- **1957: October 4** *Sputnik 1*, the world's first artificial satellite, is launched by the Soviet Union.
- **1960: April 1** *TIROS* (Television Infrared Observation Satellite) is launched.
- **1962: July 10** *Telstar 1*, the first active communications satellite, is launched by the US.
- **1963: January** First satellite navigation system, *Transit*, is launched by the US .
- **1965: April 6** The world's first geostationary satellite for commercial use, called *Early Bird*, is launched.
- **1978: June** *Seasat*, the first satellite to make valuable measurements of the oceans using radar, is launched.
- **1989: November 18** Launch of Cosmic Background Explorer Satellite.
- **1990: April 24** Hubble Space Telescope is launched.
- **1990: October 6** *Ulysses* is launched to study the Sun's polar regions.
- **1991: April 5** The Compton Gamma Ray Observatory is launched.
- **1995: December 2** *SOHO* is launched by NASA/ESA to study the Sun.
- **2002: March** *Envisat* is launched by ESA to monitor the evolution of environmental and climatic changes.

Early Space Missions

- **1957: November 3** Laika the dog becomes the first creature to orbit the Earth, inside *Sputnik 2*.
- **1961: April 12** Cosmonaut Yuri Gagarin becomes the first human in space, and the first to orbit the Earth.
- **1961: May 5** Astronaut Alan Shepard becomes the first American in space.
- **1962: February 20** John Glenn is the first US astronaut to orbit the Earth.
- **1963: June 16** Cosmonaut Valentina Tereshkova is the first woman in space.
- **1964: October 12** The first three-man crew in space, and the first live television transmission from space.
- **1965: March 18** The first space walk, performed by cosmonaut Alexei Leonov.

- **1965: March 23** The first US two-man crew to maneuver a craft in space.
- **1965: June 3** Ed White becomes the first American to walk in space.
- **1966: March 16** The first docking in space, when *Gemini 8* docks with an Aegena rocket.
- **1967: January 27** Three astronauts die in an *Apollo 1* training session.
- **1967: April 24** The first human space death. Cosmonaut Vladimir Komarov dies on reentry to the Earth.
- **1971: June 29** Three cosmonauts die in a *Soyuz 11* capsule.
- **1975: July 17** The *Apollo-Soyuz Project*: US and Soviet spacecraft dock together for the first time.

Moon Missions

UNCREWED MISSIONS

Name	Country	Type	Launch Date	Arrival Date	Achievements
Luna 2	SU	impact	1959, Sept. 12	1959, Sept. 13	first probe to reach the Moon, crash-lands on the lunar surface
Luna 3	SU	flyby	1959, Oct. 4	1959, Oct. 6	returns first photographs of the Moon's far side, showing highlands
Ranger 7	US	impact	1964, July 28	1964, July 31	takes over 4,300 images of the surface, showing many small craters
Luna 9	SU	lander	1966, Jan. 31	1966, Feb. 3	first successful landing, takes panoramic photos of the surface
Luna 10	SU	orbiter	1966, Mar. 31	1966, Apr. 3	first spacecraft to orbit the Moon
Surveyor 1	US	lander	1966, May 30	1966, June 2	first true soft landing on the Moon
Lunar Orbiter 1	US	orbiter	1966, Aug. 10	1966, Aug. 14	takes a photo survey of the surface for potential Apollo landing sites
Zond 5	SU	flyby	1968, Sept. 15	1968, Sept. 18	first flight to orbit the Moon and return to Earth
Luna 17	SU	rover	1970, Nov. 10	1970, Nov. 17	delivers *Lunokhod 1*, the first rover to drive on the Moon
Clementine	US	orbiter	1994, Jan. 25	1994, Feb. 21	surveys the surface mineralogy of the Moon at high resolution
Lunar Prospector	US	orbiter	1998, Jan. 7	1998, Jan. 11	surveys the composition of the Moon, finds ice in the polar craters

CREWED MISSIONS

Name	Country	Launch Date	Arrival Date	Achievements
Apollo 8	US	1968, Dec. 21	1968, Dec. 24	first crewed craft to leave Earth's orbit, first to orbit the Moon
Apollo 9	US	1969, Mar. 3	N/A	crewed test of lunar hardware in Earth's orbit
Apollo 10	US	1969, May 18	1969, May 22	a "dry run" for the *Apollo 11* mission
Apollo 11	US	1969, July 16	1969, July 20	Neil Armstrong and Buzz Aldrin are the first men to set foot on the Moon
Apollo 12	US	1969, Nov. 14	1969, Nov. 19	scientific experiments set up, photographs taken, samples collected
Apollo 13	US	1970, Apr. 11	1970, Apr. 14	a liquid oxygen tank explodes, landing aborted, crew returns safely
Apollo 14	US	1972, Jan. 31	1971, Feb. 5	third manned mission to land on the Moon
Apollo 15	US	1971, July 26	1971, July 30	Lunar Roving Vehicle is used for the first time
Apollo 16	US	1972, Apr. 16	1972, Apr. 21	scientific experiments set up, photographs taken, samples collected
Apollo 17	US	1972, Dec. 7	1972, Dec. 11	last mission to land humans on the Moon

Planetary Missions

	Name	Country	Type	Launch Date	Arrival Date	Achievements
Mercury	Mariner 10	US	flyby	1973, Nov. 3	1974, Mar. 29	first close-up images of the planet's cratered surface
Venus	Mariner 2	US	flyby	1962, Aug. 27	1962, Dec. 14	first probe to fly by another planet
	Venera 4	SU	lander	1967, June 12	1967, Oct. 18	first Venera probe to successfully transmit data
	Venera 7	SU	lander	1970, Aug. 17	1970, Dec. 15	first spacecraft to transmit data from the surface of another planet
	Venera 9	SU	lander	1975, June 8	1975, Oct. 22	transmits first photos of the Venusian surface
	Pioneer 1	US	orbiter	1978, May 20	1978, Dec. 4	takes first global radar map
	Magellan	US	orbiter	1989, May 4	1990, Aug. 10	maps the planet using radar
Mars	Mariner 4	US	flyby	1964, Nov. 28	1965, July 14	first craft to fly by Mars, first close-up images of the surface
	Mars 3	SU	lander	1971, May 28	1971, Dec. 3	first landing on the surface, but signals cease after 20 seconds
	Mariner 9	US	orbiter	1971, May 30	1971, Nov. 14	first craft to orbit another planet, surveys entire surface
	Viking 1	US	lander	1975, Aug. 20	1976, June 19	first craft to land successfully and fully function on Mars
	Viking 2	US	lander	1975, Sept. 9	1976, Aug. 7	analyzes the rocks, and searches (unsuccessfully) for life
	Global Surveyor	US	orbiter	1996, Nov. 7	1997, Sept. 11	maps the entire planet at high resolution
	Pathfinder	US	lander	1996, Dec. 2	1997, July 4	explores geology of a once-flooded landscape
Jupiter	Pioneer 10	US	flyby	1972, Mar. 3	1973, Dec. 3	first flyby and first detailed study of a gas giant
	Pioneer 11	US	flyby	1973, Apr. 6	1974, Dec. 3	studies the polar regions of Jupiter
	Voyager 1	US	flyby	1977, Sept. 5	1979, Mar. 5	first detailed images of planet and moons, discovers ring system
	Voyager 2	US	flyby	1977, Aug. 20	1979, July 9	followup on the discoveries made by *Voyager 1*
	Galileo	US	entry	1989, Oct. 18	1995, Dec. 7	sends probe into Jupiter's atmosphere, begins tour of the moons
	Cassini	US	flyby	1997, Oct. 15	2000, Dec. 30	first close-up images of the planet's cratered surface
Saturn	Pioneer 11	US	flyby	1973, Apr. 6	1979, Sept. 1	first craft to fly by Saturn, discovers new rings
	Voyager 1	US	flyby	1977, Sept. 5	1980, Nov. 12	first detailed study of Saturn system
	Voyager 2	US	flyby	1977, Aug. 20	1981, Aug. 25	takes detailed portraits of clouds, rings, and moons
	Cassini	US	flyby	1997, Oct. 15	2004, July	tour of the planet and moons, will deliver a lander for Titan
Uranus	Voyager 2	US	flyby	1977, Aug. 20	1986, Jan. 24	first flyby, studies rings and moons and finds new moons
Neptune	Voyager 2	US	flyby	1977, Aug. 20	1989, Aug. 25	first flyby of Neptune and its moons, studies storms and finds geysers on Triton

Space Stations and Shuttles

- **1971: April 19** Launch of the world's first space station, the Soviet *Salyut 1*.
- **1973: May 14** The first US space station, *Skylab*, is launched.
- **1977: September 29** Launch of *Salyut 6*, the first station to have two docking facilities.
- **1982: April 19** *Salyut 7*, the last in the Soviet Salyut series, is launched.
- **1981: April 12** Launch of the first US space shuttle, *Columbia*.

- **1986: January 28** US space shuttle *Challenger* explodes, killing crew of seven.
- **1986: February 20** Launch of Soviet *Mir* space station.
- **1988: November 20** Launch of the first module of the *International Space Station*.
- **2003: February 1** US space shuttle *Columbia* disintegrates, killing crew of seven.

The space shuttle is launched to take a module to the ISS

Moon Landings

BETWEEN 1969 AND 1972, six Apollo missions successfully landed on the Moon, and 12 men walked on its surface. They explored over 60 miles (100 km) of the lunar surface and returned 880 lb (400 kg) of rocks and soil to Earth.

North

MARE IMBRIUM (Sea of Rains)

Apollo 15

MARE SERENITATIS (Sea of Serenity)

Apollo 17

OCEANUS PROCELLARUM (Ocean of Storms)

Crater Kepler

Crater Copernicus

MARE TRANQUILLITATIS (Sea of Tranquillity)

Apollo 11

NECTARIS (Sea of Nectar)

Apollo 12

Apollo 14

Apollo 16

MARE COGNITUM (Known Sea)

MARE HUMORUM (Sea of Moisture)

MARE NUBIUM (Sea of Clouds)

Crater Tycho

South

About the Moon

- Diameter: 2,158 miles (3,476 km)
- Average distance from Earth: 239,000 miles (384,400 km)
- Time of orbit around Earth: 27.3 days
- The Moon's far side is hidden from us; it orbits with one face locked toward Earth.
- The lunar surface is made of anorthosite (basaltlike rock), covered with craters.
- The Moon is made up of three layers: an outer crust, an inner mantle and a central core.
- The dark "seas," called maria, are not seas at all. They are impact craters from about 4 billion years ago. Several hundred million years later, lava oozed through the Moon's crust to flood them.

APOLLO 11	APOLLO 12	APOLLO 14

APOLLO 11

LANDING SITE: Mare Tranquillitatis (Sea of Tranquillity) CREW: Commander Neil A. Armstrong, Command Module Pilot Michael Collins, Lunar Module Pilot Edwin "Buzz" Aldrin LANDED ON MOON: July 20, 1969 TIME ON SURFACE: 21 hours, 38 minutes

The first crewed mission to land on the Moon and to return samples from another planetary body.

APOLLO 12

LANDING SITE: Edge of Oceanus Procellarum (Ocean of Storms) CREW: Commander Charles Conrad, Jr., Command Module Pilot Richard F. Gordon, Lunar Module Pilot Alan L. Bean LANDED ON MOON: November 19, 1969 TIME ON SURFACE: 31 hours, 31 minutes

The Saturn rocket was hit by lightning twice just after launch, temporarily cutting off electrical power.

APOLLO 14

LANDING SITE: Crater Fra Mauro CREW: Commander Alan B. Shepard, Command Module Pilot Stuart A. Roosa, Lunar Module Pilot Edgar D. Mitchell LANDED ON MOON: February 5, 1971 TIME ON SURFACE: 33 hours, 31 minutes

Apollo 14 almost failed to leave the Moon; it took six attempts to dock the lunar module with the orbiting command and service modules.

en on the Moon

Only 12 human beings have ever walked on the Moon—all men. Neil Armstrong was the first, in 1969, and Eugene Cernan the last in 1972, just three years later. Every Apollo crew consisted of three astronauts. The command module pilot remained in lunar orbit while the other two astronauts descended in the lunar module.

- The men had to undergo extreme physical and mental fitness tests such as heat, stress, and vibration tolerance.

- Harrison Schmitt of the *Apollo 17* mission was the only trained scientist to visit the Moon.

- Between them, the Apollo astronauts set up over 50 experiments on six sites on the Moon's surface.

- The *Apollo 11* landing was one of the first events ever to be broadcast live by satellite all over the world.

Apollo 11 crew (left to right) Neil Armstrong, Michael Collins, Buzz Aldrin

MARE CRISIUM (Sea of Crises)

MARE FECUNDITATIS (Sea of Fecundity)

Mighty Saturn V Rocket

All the crewed Apollo missions were launched on a Saturn V rocket, designed by Wernher von Braun, who named all his rockets after planets. The Saturn V stood 363 ft (110.6 m) tall—as high as a 36-story building. It weighed more than 6 million lb (2.7 million kg).

- The Saturn V rocket was made up of three stages. Each contained one or more engines, a fuel tank, and a liquid oxygen tank.

- Five engines powered the first stage of the rocket, giving the vehicle its 'V' (five) designation.

- The crewed Apollo craft was situated at the top of the launch vehicle.

- The Apollo spacecraft consisted of a command module, service module, and lunar module.

- Reaching a speed of 7 miles/sec (11 km/s), the rocket was able to escape Earth's gravity.

Launch Escape Tower

Command Module

Third Stage: contained one engine that took the craft to orbital velocity.

Second Stage: took rocket up 77 miles (124 km) after first stage separated.

First Stage: five engines, the most powerful ever built, lifted rocket from launch pad.

APOLLO 15

LANDING SITE: Hadley Rille/Apennines
CREW: Commander David R. Scott, Command Module Pilot Alfred M. Worden, Service Module Pilot James B. Irwin
LANDED ON MOON: July 30, 1971
TIME ON SURFACE: 66 hours, 54 minutes

The first mission to use an LRV (lunar roving vehicle). It could carry two astronauts plus scientific equipment, tools, and communications gear.

APOLLO 16

LANDING SITE: Descartes
CREW: Commander John W. Young, Command Module Pilot Thomas K. Mattingly II, Lunar Module Pilot Charles M. Duke, Jr.
LANDED ON MOON: April 20, 1972
TIME ON SURFACE: 71 hours, 2 minutes

Landed in a previously unexplored highlands area. Crew conducted many experiments, including the first use of an ultraviolet camera on the Moon.

APOLLO 17

LANDING SITE: Taurus-Littrow Valley
CREW: Commander Eugene A. Cernan, Command Module Pilot Ronald E. Evans, Lunar Module Pilot Harrison H. Schmitt
LANDED ON MOON: December 11, 1972
TIME ON SURFACE: 75 hours

The LRV traveled 18.6 miles (30 km) on the Moon. A record amount of rock samples was returned to Earth—242 lb (110 kg).

Spacecraft

ALL SPACECRAFT have to be launched from the
Earth by rocket. There are many types of space
vehicles: some are crewed by astronauts, some
explore a planetary surface, and others orbit or
fly by planets while gathering information.

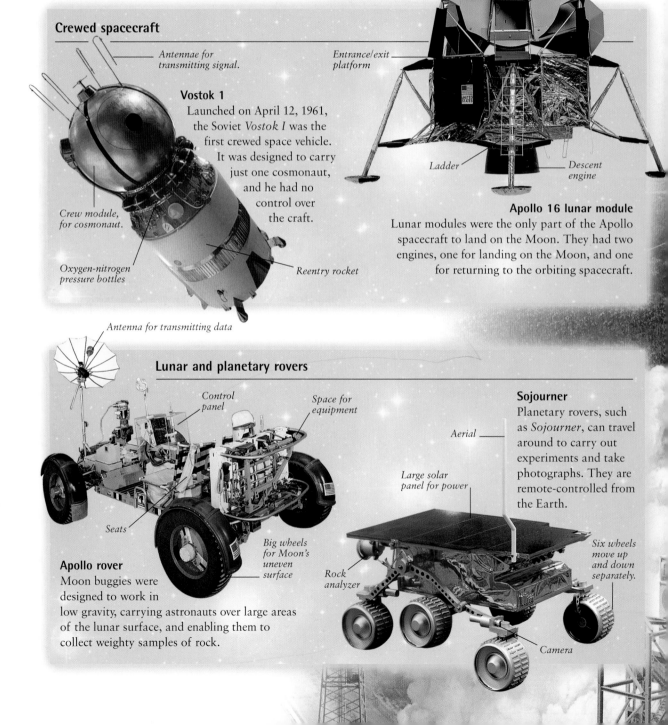

Rendezvous
radar

Window

Tracking light

Crew hatch

Crewed spacecraft

Antennae for
transmitting signal.

Entrance/exit
platform

Vostok 1
Launched on April 12, 1961,
the Soviet *Vostok I* was the
first crewed space vehicle.
It was designed to carry
just one cosmonaut,
and he had no
control over
the craft.

Crew module,
for cosmonaut.

Oxygen-nitrogen
pressure bottles

Reentry rocket

Ladder

Descent
engine

Apollo 16 lunar module
Lunar modules were the only part of the Apollo
spacecraft to land on the Moon. They had two
engines, one for landing on the Moon, and one
for returning to the orbiting spacecraft.

Antenna for transmitting data

Lunar and planetary rovers

Control
panel

Space for
equipment

Aerial

Sojourner
Planetary rovers, such
as *Sojourner*, can travel
around to carry out
experiments and take
photographs. They are
remote-controlled from
the Earth.

Large solar
panel for power

Seats

Big wheels
for Moon's
uneven
surface

Rock
analyzer

Six wheels
move up
and down
separately.

Apollo rover
Moon buggies were
designed to work in
low gravity, carrying astronauts over large areas
of the lunar surface, and enabling them to
collect weighty samples of rock.

Camera

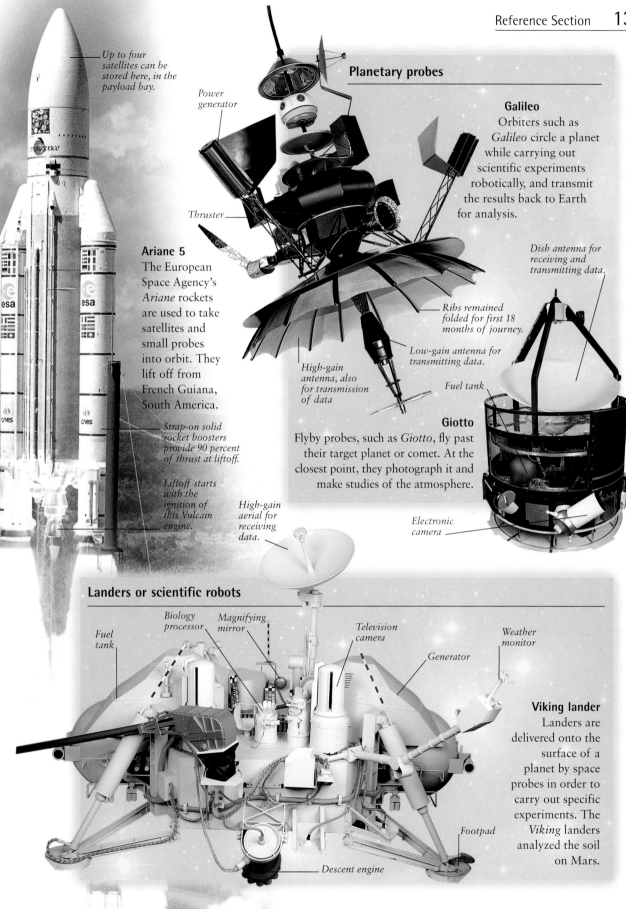

Up to four satellites can be stored here, in the payload bay.

Planetary probes

Power generator

Thruster

Galileo
Orbiters such as *Galileo* circle a planet while carrying out scientific experiments robotically, and transmit the results back to Earth for analysis.

Dish antenna for receiving and transmitting data.

Ariane 5
The European Space Agency's *Ariane* rockets are used to take satellites and small probes into orbit. They lift off from French Guiana, South America.

Ribs remained folded for first 18 months of journey.

Strap-on solid rocket boosters provide 90 percent of thrust at liftoff.

Low-gain antenna for transmitting data.

High-gain antenna, also for transmission of data

Fuel tank

Giotto
Flyby probes, such as *Giotto*, fly past their target planet or comet. At the closest point, they photograph it and make studies of the atmosphere.

Liftoff starts with the ignition of this Vulcain engine.

High-gain aerial for receiving data.

Electronic camera

Landers or scientific robots

Fuel tank

Biology processor

Magnifying mirror

Television camera

Generator

Weather monitor

Viking lander
Landers are delivered onto the surface of a planet by space probes in order to carry out specific experiments. The *Viking* landers analyzed the soil on Mars.

Footpad

Descent engine

Stars

Core is where nuclear reactions generate the star's energy.

Radiation zone is where heat radiates out from the star's center.

Convection zone is where hot gases circulate the heat.

Photosphere is the bright shining surface of the star.

Cross-section of a "red giant" star.

The tiny stars twinkling in the night sky are actually huge, fiery balls of gas. They are born inside clouds of gas and dust known as nebulas. The gas swirls, heats up, and shrinks into shining balls—stars—that shine for billions of years before swelling and dying. Stars come in many different sizes, from tiny "white dwarfs" roughly the size of Earth, through average-sized stars such as our Sun (known as main sequence stars), to huge "red giants" and massive "supergiants."

- The closest star to Earth is Proxima Centauri, a red dwarf star, which lies 4.2 light-years away.
- The brightest star in our night sky is Sirius, in the constellation Canis Major, 8.6 light-years away.

Space Facts

OUR PLANET EARTH is one of nine planets that orbit a fiery star called the Sun. Beyond our Solar System of planets, moons, and Sun lie all the stars we see in our night sky. They are part of our galaxy, the Milky Way. But our galaxy is just one of billions of galaxies, each containing billions of stars. Together these galaxies make up the Universe.

JUPITER
The largest planet in our Solar System, Jupiter has 317.8 times the mass of Earth and about 11 times its diameter.

COMPARATIVE SIZES OF PLANETS

Shown here, in order and with relative sizes, are the nine planets of our Solar System. Near the Sun are the rocky planets of Mercury, Venus, Earth, and Mars. Farther out lie the gas giants, Jupiter, Saturn, Uranus and Neptune. Farther still is tiny Pluto.

MERCURY
The fastest-moving planet, it orbits the Sun at 30 miles/sec (48 km/s).

VENUS
The hottest of the planets, Venus's thick atmosphere holds in the Sun's heat.

EARTH
The only planet in the Solar System that has the necessary conditions to support life.

MARS
The color of Mars's surface is caused by the same chemical that makes rust red—iron oxide.

DISTANCES FROM THE SUN

The line to the right shows the distances of the planets from the Sun. A planet's "year" is the time it takes to travel around (orbit) the Sun. Planets farther from the Sun have longer years.

Mercury Venus Earth Mars   Jupiter   Saturn

| 0 | 310 million miles (500 million km) | 620 (1,000) | 930 (1,500) | 1,240 (2,000) |

Galaxies

A cloud of gas shrinks, becoming hotter and denser, and stars begin to form. These stars cluster together to form a new galaxy, which begins to spin. The birth rate, spin speed, and contents of a galaxy all determine its shape. Our home galaxy, the Milky Way, is a spiral shape. Our Solar System sits on one of the spiral arms that curl out from the bulging galactic center. The Milky Way contains as many as 200 billion stars.

Elliptical Galaxies
These ball- or egg-shaped galaxies contain mainly old stars. More than half of all known galaxies are ellipticals.

Spiral Galaxies
"Arms" of young stars extend out from a center, or nucleus, of older stars, to create beautiful spiral galaxies.

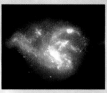

Irregular Galaxies
Galaxies with no definite shape are known as irregular. They often contain a large amount of gas and dust.

PLUTO
The smallest planet, only discovered in 1930. We will not know Pluto's coldest temperature until 2114, when it will reach its farthest point from the Sun.

NEPTUNE
The last of the gas giants, Neptune has the most violent weather of all the nine planets. Its winds can reach speeds of up to 1,250 mph (2,000 km/h).

URANUS
Discovered in 1781 by William Herschel, this planet has 10 rings and a mass 14.5 times that of Earth.

SATURN
This planet takes over 29 years to orbit the Sun. It can be seen from Earth with the naked eye, but its rings are visible only through a telescope.

Solar System Facts

	Diameter miles (km)	Mass Earth=1	Avg. surface temp. °F (°C)	Solar day	Length of year in Earth days	Number of moons	Number of rings	Number of probe visits
SUN	865,000 (1,392,000)	332,946	9,900 (5,500)	—	—	—	—	—
MERCURY	3,029 (4,875)	0.055	333 (167)	176 Earth days	88	0	0	1
VENUS	7,521 (12,104)	0.082	880 (470)	117 Earth days	225	0	0	31
EARTH	7,918 (12,785)	1	63 (17)	24 hr	365.25	1	0	n/a
MARS	4,213 (6,780)	0.064	-74 (-59)	24 hr, 37 min	687	2	0	23
JUPITER	88,846 (142,984)	317.8	-166 (-110)	9 hr, 55 min	4,331	61	3	5
SATURN	74,896 (120,533)	95.2	-220 (-140)	10 hr, 39 min	10,747	31	7	4
URANUS	31,763 (51,118)	14.5	-319 (-195)	17 hr, 14 min	30,589	21	11	1
NEPTUNE	30,775 (49,528)	17.2	-328 (-200)	16 hr, 7 min	59,800	11	6	1
PLUTO	1,432 (2,304)	0.002	-373 (-225)	6.4 Earth days	90,588	1	0	0

Glossary

Words in *italics* have their own entry in the glossary.

A

Alloy A mixture of metals, or of a metal and a nonmetal.

Arms race When two nations compete to have more powerful weapons than one another. The *Cold War* led to an arms race between the US and the *Soviet Union*. (See also *Space race*)

Asteroid A large chunk of rock in the *Solar System*, sometimes called a minor *planet*. Most asteroids lie in a belt around the *Sun* between Mars and Jupiter.

Atmosphere A layer of gas held by *gravity* around a *planet*, *moon*, or *star*.

Atmospheric friction The resistance of Earth's *atmosphere* on a *spacecraft* that is traveling back to Earth. This friction generates intense heat, so spacecraft must be coated with protective heat shields.

Aurora Green and red glow seen in the sky near the polar regions; known as aurora borealis or northern lights in the north, and aurora australis or southern lights in the south. Auroras are caused by electrically charged particles colliding with gases in the Earth's *atmosphere*.

B

Big Bang The theory that a violent explosion gave birth to the *Universe* about 14 billion years ago.

Binary stars *See double stars*

Black hole A region of space where *gravity* is so strong that nothing, not even light, can escape from it.

C

Capitalism An economic system under which most land and wealth is owned by private individuals. Most countries, including the United States, favor this system. (*See also Communism*)

Carbon One of the most common *elements* in the *Universe*. Carbon is the basis of all life on Earth.

Celestial body Any natural object seen in the sky, including *planets*, *stars*, and *galaxies*.

Cluster *See Galaxy cluster* or *Star cluster*.

Cold War The political and military rivalry between the United States and the *Soviet Union* from about 1945–92.

Comet An object made of ice and dust within our *Solar System* that orbits the *Sun*. When a comet nears the Sun, the Sun's heat vaporizes the ice, creating a glowing head (coma) with tails of dust and gas.

Command Module *See Module.*

Communism An economic system in which the government owns land and wealth. This system operated in the *Soviet Union*. (*See also Capitalism*)

Cosmonaut A Russian astronaut.

D

Diameter A straight line through the center of a circle or a sphere that represents how wide it is.

Docking The process by which two *modules* join together.

Double stars A pair of *stars* that orbit around one another, also known as binary stars.

E

Electromagnetic radiation Waves of energy that can travel through space and (sometimes) through matter. They range from *gamma rays* (shortest *wavelength*) through *ultraviolet*, visible light, and *infrared*, to radio waves (longest wavelength).

Element Any of the roughly one hundred basic substances in nature that cannot be broken down by chemical reactions. Each element has its own unique properties.

Escape velocity The speed at which a *rocket* or *spacecraft* must travel to escape the *gravity* of a *celestial body*. A speed of 7 miles/sec (11 km/s) is needed to escape from Earth.

EVA Stands for extravehicular activity, and refers to spacewalks performed by *astronauts* while outside of their *spacecraft*.

F G

Flyby An encounter between a space *probe* and a *planet*, *comet* or *asteroid*, in which the probe does not stop to orbit or land.

Galaxy A huge *star* system containing millions or billions of stars, as well as clouds of gas and dust, held together by *gravity*.

Galaxy cluster Group of galaxies held together by gravity.

Gamma rays *Electromagnetic radiation* with very short *wavelengths* emitted by the most energetic objects in the *Universe*.

Geiger counter An instrument to measure and detect *radioactivity*.

Globular cluster *See Star cluster*.

Gravity Force of attraction between any objects with mass, such as the pull between the Earth and the *Moon*.

H

Helium The second-lightest and second most common *element* in the *Universe*, produced in the *Big Bang* and by *nuclear reactions* in *stars*.

Hydrogen The most common and lightest *element* in the *Universe*—the main component of *stars*, *galaxies*, and giant *planets*.

I

Infrared *Electromagnetic radiation* with *wavelengths* just longer than visible light, it can be felt as heat. Infrared cameras and telescopes are used to detect invisible *celestial bodies*.

Interplanetary Between planets.

Interstellar Between stars.

K L

Kuiper belt An area of the *Solar System*, located beyond the orbit of Pluto, containing millions of icy, cometlike objects.

Lander A *probe* built to land on a *planet*, *moon*, or *asteroid*, to investigate the surface.

Laser A device that produces an intense beam of pure light (of a single *wavelength*).

Launch pad A platform from which a *rocket* can be launched.

Lava Molten rock released from the inside of a *planet* or *moon* onto the surface.

Light-year The distance light travels in one year, roughly 6 trillion miles (9.5 trillion km).

Lunar module *See module.*

Lunar rover Used on Apollo missions 15–17, this vehicle allowed a greater amount of the Moon's surface to be explored.

M

Mach A measurement of speed; Mach 1 is the speed of sound, anything that can travel faster than Mach 1 is *supersonic*.

Magnetic field Field of force that exists around a magnetic body.

Meteor Streak of light across the sky caused by a speck of rock (usually *comet* dust) burning up as it enters Earth's *atmosphere*. Also known as a shooting star.

Meteoroid Fragments of rock and dust from *asteroids* and *comets* in space.

Meteorite A *meteoroid* that has fallen onto the surface of a *planet* or *moon*. The impact as it hits the surface may smash it into bits and also form a crater.

Microgravity Very low *gravity*, as experienced by astronauts in *orbit*. Microgravity is a more accurate term than zero gravity. This is because a *spacecraft's* movements are usually creating gravity in one direction.

Milky Way The name given to the *galaxy* in which we live.

Missile A weapon capable of being launched on a *rocket*.

Module A part of a *spacecraft*. Apollo spacecraft contained three modules: a lunar module (LM) that landed on the Moon, a command module (CM) from which the astronauts controlled the craft, and a service module (SM) that provided oxygen, water and power.

Moon A *planet*'s natural *satellite*. Earth's satellite is called the Moon but those of other planets have unique names, such as Jupiter's moon, Io.

N

NASA Stands for the National Aeronautics and Space Administration. This US organization was set up in 1958 to conduct civilian aeronautical and space research.

Nebula A cloud of gas and dust in space. Nebulas are visible when they reflect starlight or when they block out light coming from behind them.

Northern lights *See Aurora*

Nuclear reaction The energy source of *stars*. By fusing simple *elements* into more complex ones, huge amounts of energy are released.

O

Open cluster *See Star cluster*

Orbit The path of one object around another object controlled by the influence of *gravity*, such as that of the *Moon* around the Earth, and the Earth around the *Sun*.

Orbital velocity The speed needed to keep a *spacecraft* in *orbit* around a *planet* or *moon* without it falling to the surface.

Orbiter A *spacecraft* or *satellite* that *orbits* a *planet* or *moon* without landing on it.

P

Payload Cargo carried into space by a *rocket*.

Planet A large, spherical object made of rock or gas that orbits the *Sun* or another *star*. Planets do not produce their own light, but reflect the light of the star.

Planetary rings Ring-shaped structures composed of small bodies of dust, rock, or ice surrounding Jupiter, Saturn, Uranus, and Neptune.

Photosphere A *star*'s visible surface, from which its light shines out into space.

Probe An uncrewed *spacecraft* containing instruments for space exploration and investigation.

Propaganda The organized spreading of information, either true or false, often with the aim of influencing the public.

Propellant The fuel used in *rocket* engines and needed to force a rocket to move forward. Propellants can be in either a solid or a liquid form.

Q R

Quasar A distant *galaxy* that releases enormous amounts of energy from its small center. Quasars are some of the most distant galaxies in the *Universe*.

Radiation Energy traveling as *electromagnetic* waves (such as light). Also, the rays given off by radioactive substances, such as alpha, beta, and gamma rays.

Radioactivity Breakdown of the nucleus (center) of certain *elements* through a process of *nuclear reaction*, causing energy to be released as *radiation*.

Reconnaissance The inspection and exploration of an area to discover information.

Ring *See planetary rings*.

Rocket A vehicle powered by rocket engines, used to get a *spacecraft* into space. The spacecraft sits at the top of the rocket.

S

Satellite An object held in orbit around another object by *gravity*. Natural satellites are called *moons*.

Seismograph An instrument for registering earthquakes.

Service module *See module*.

Solar radiation The energy emitted from the Sun in the form of *electromagnetic radiation*— mainly light and heat.

Solar System The *Sun* and all the *planets*, *moons*, *asteroids*, *comets*, and *meteoroids* that orbit the Sun due to *gravity*. The Sun is the only *star* in our Solar System.

Solar wind A stream of high-speed atomic particles that blows away from the Sun.

Sound barrier *See supersonic*.

Soviet Union A former communist country in eastern Europe and northern Asia that was established in 1922 and collapsed in 1992. It included Russia and 14 other republics.

Spacecraft A vehicle, either crewed or uncrewed, that is put into space to explore *planets*, *moons*, *asteroids*, and *comets*. Spacecraft can be *landers*, *orbiters*, or *flyby* vehicles.

Space probe *See probe*.

Space race The *Cold War* extended to space exploration. The US and the Soviet Union raced one another to be the first to demonstrate impressive feats of rocketry and spaceflight.

Space shuttle *NASA*'s reusable *spacecraft* that carries people and *payload* into *orbit* around the Earth.

Space station A large *spacecraft* that *orbits* the Earth and is occupied for long periods by astronauts. Astronauts perform many scientific experiments while on board.

Spacewalk *See EVA*.

Star A hot, massive, luminous ball of gas that makes energy in its core from *nuclear reactions*.

Star cluster Group of *stars* held together by *gravity*. Open clusters are loose groups of a few hundred young stars. Globular clusters are dense balls containing many thousands of old stars.

Suborbital flight When a *spacecraft* travels along a *trajectory* of less than one *orbit*.

Sun The central *star* of the *Solar System*. The Sun is an average-sized star.

Supernova An enormous explosion that occurs when a massive *star* known as a supergiant runs out of fuel and dies.

Supersonic Traveling faster than the speed of sound. To reach these high speeds requires breaking through the sound barrier.

T

Technology When science is used in a practical and industrial way.

Trajectory The path a moving object travels along.

Transmitter Instrument used to broadcast information, usually via radio waves.

U

Ultrasound Sound waves that are too high in frequency to be heard by human ears.

Ultraviolet Invisible *electromagnetic radiation* with a shorter *wavelength* than visible light. UV rays in sunlight can burn the skin.

Universe Everything that exists— from *comets*, *asteroids* and *meteoroids*, through *moons* and *planets*, to stars and *galaxies*.

V W

Velocity Speed of an object in a particular direction.

Warhead The part of a missile that contains the explosive.

Warp-drive The term given to faster-than-light travel. Current scientific knowledge claims that this is impossible, since it would require an infinite amount of energy to reach such speeds.

Wavelength Distance between the peaks or troughs in waves of *electromagnetic radiation*.

X Z

X-rays *Electromagnetic radiation* with a very short *wavelength* produced by extremely hot gas clouds and stars, and around black holes.

Zero gravity *See Microgravity*.

Index

Acknowledgments

The publisher would like to thank the following for their kind permission to reproduce their photographs: (Abbreviations key: t=top, b=bottom, r=right, l=left, c=center)

AKG London: 29tcr, Giotto de Bonsome 110cl, Giotto di Bondone 108crb; **Corbis**: Bettman 3cbl, 15crb, 17crb, 19clb, 34bl, 36bl, 41br, 40-41, 99clb, 102cla, 102clb, 138cl, 7cbl, 10-11, Marc Garanger 21ca, Anne Hawthorne 128-129, 77tr; Hulton-Deutsch 12bl, 45br, 77tr, Yevgeny Khaldeny 36tl, 23, 38tl, 69clb, Magellan/NASAJPL/Roger Ressmeyer 19cb, 24bc, 31cb, 42-43, 43cra, 49crb, 106tc, NASA 45tr, David Samuel Robbins 16tl, Caroline Penn 128bc, Rykoff Collection 134cla, Dennis Scott 79clb, 82-83, 88tc, Ted Streshinsky 31clb, The Mariners' Museum 24tr; **European Space Agency**: 43crb, 77br, JPL/NASA 140cr, 110crb, CNE/Arianespace-Service 139tl;

London Planetarium: 135clb, 141c, NASA 15cra, 111cr, 113tr, 138clb; Science Museum: 39tr, 139cb; **Genesis Space Photo Library**: 25br, NASA 27tr, 83tr, 103c; **NASA**: 1cl, 2cra, 2bl, 2br, 2bcr, 3bc, 3bcl, 4, 5bl, 6, 8cl, 8, 10bl, 14tl, 14-15, 21tr, 24-25, 26, 28, 30crb, 33tr, 35tc, 37bl, 37, 42tl, 44tl, 46crb, 46-47, 47clb, 47cb, 48cla, 49br, 51tr, 54tc, 54-55, 55br, 56crb, 57clb, 58tc, 59br, 60tl, 61ca, 61cra, 61, 61cal, 61car, 62tc, 62c, 62, 65tc, 65crb, 65br, 66tl, 66clb, 67, 69cb, 70bl, 71tc, 71clb, 71, 71-72, 74cl, 75bc, 76bl, 78crb, 78-79, 80-81, 88tl, 88crb, 89clb, 90tl, 90cla, 90-91, 92tl, 92tr, 92clb, 93tr, 94-95, 95bc, 95br, 98crb, 98-99, 99cb, 100tl, 101tr, 101crb, 102cl, 104bl, 105tr, 106bl, 107tl, 107br, 109ca, 109clb, 111, 112-113, 115bc, 116-117, 125bc, 126-127, 128tl, 128cr, 130cb, 130bc, 132tl, 132bc, 134cra, 134-135, 135bl, 135bc, 135br, 136clb, 136cb, 136crb, 137cl, 137clb, 137cb, 137crb, Johnson Space Center 81cra, JPL 89cb, 96tc, JPL/Caltech 84-85, 85cr, 86cla, 20bl, 35br, 57clb, 75tr, 119cb, 120,

SOHO 109cb, TRACE 116clb; **National Space Development of Japan**: 142-143; **NOAO/AURA/NSF/WIYN**: 4-5; **Novosti (London)**: 3bl, 11crb, 20tc, 26cl, 29br, 32cl, 68; **Popperfoto**: 7cb, 16-17, 25cr, 71bc; **Rex Features**: 127clb, 130tl, SNAP agency 29tc, 29cra; **Royalty Free Images/Corbis**: 3br, 126-127; **Science Photo Library**: Andrew Macfadyen 115cra, Julian Baum 125tc, Chris Butler 131bc, Martin Dohron 82bl, David Duicros 97crb, E R Degginger 77tl, Jack Finch 70tl, Victor Habbick 127cb, 133,Tony & Daphne Hallas 3cbr; 108-109, 140cla, 141ca, 141car, David Hardy 89cb, 96cla, Harvard College Observatory 110tl, Joe Lomberg 131c, 96tl, Max Planck Institute for Radio Astrology 22c, NASA 3bcr, 68crb, 72tl, 73tc, 74tl, 79cb, 86-87, 118, 19clb, 122bc, 123tr, 123crb, 131cra, 134cb, 135cla, 137cra, 138br, 140tc, 140cbl, NOAO 141ca, Novosti 2bc, 19cra, 20br, 30-31, 32bl, Royal Edinburgh Observatory/AAO 115tl,136-137,138-139; Space Telescope

Science Inst./NASA 114, 135cl, 141cra, 141cl, John Sanford 89cb, 96tl, Dr Seth Shostak 129tr, Eckhard Slawik 114c, Geoff Tompkinson 129crb, Joe Tucciaron 132clb, US Geological Survey 84tc, Frank Zullo 136ca; **Calvin J Hamilton/Solarviews.com**: 97tr; **Getty Images**: Image Bank 94clb; **Topham Picturepoint**: 2bcl, 18-19; **Verena Tunnicliffe**: 124tl.

All other images © Dorling Kindersley
For further information see:
www.dkimages.com

Dorling Kindersley would also like to thank:

DK Picture Librarians Sarah Mills, Carl Strange and Gemma Woodward; Kate Bradshaw, Fran Jones, Bradley Round, and Kate Turner for editorial assistance; Leah Germann and Floyd Sayers for design assistance; Mark Walker for digital artwork; Alyson Lacewing for proofreading; Chris Bernstein for the index.